F

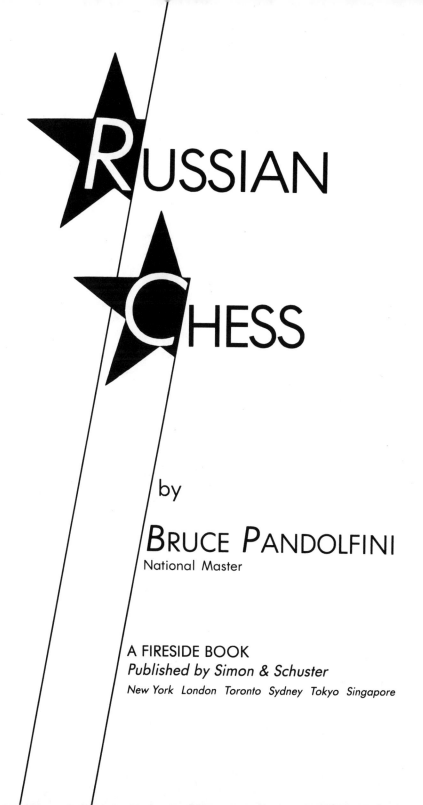

RUSSIAN

CHESS

by

BRUCE PANDOLFINI
National Master

A FIRESIDE BOOK
Published by Simon & Schuster
New York London Toronto Sydney Tokyo Singapore

A Fireside Book
Published by Simon & Schuster, Inc.
Simon & Schuster Building
Rockefeller Center
1230 Avenue of the Americas
New York, New York 10020

FIRESIDE and colophon are registered trademarks of Simon & Schuster, Inc.

Designed by Stanley S. Drate/Folio Graphics Company, Inc.

Manufactured in the United States of America

10 9 8 7 6 5

Library of Congress Cataloging in Publication Data

Pandolfini, Bruce.
   Russian chess.

   "A Fireside book."
   1. Chess—Miscellanea.   I. Title.
GV1449.5.P36   1987   794.1   86-22901

ISBN: 0-671-61984-5

CONTENTS

For Red

I would like to thank Idelle Pandolfini for her insightful editing and suggestions; Carol Ann Caronia for her intelligent criticism; America's preeminent chess historian, master Bruce Alberston, for his prodigious research, analysis, and technical virtuosity; masters Larry Tamarkin and Alan Kantor for their diagramming; Roane Carey and Nick Swyrydenko for their reliable, conscientious editing and advice; and general editor Deborah Bergman for her invaluable contributions to the manuscript at every stage of its production.

INTRODUCTION

Russian Chess is an instructional book based on six chess games played in the past few years by the rousing new generation of Soviet grandmasters. Each chapter examines several vital themes in contemporary chess through in-depth discussion, with questions and answers that painstakingly guide the reader through the vicissitudes of each game. The entire six lessons represent a complete course in modern chess logic—showing how moves, plans, and strategies are formulated.

There are good reasons for a new book on Russian chess. Since 1927, the Russians have consistently held the world title (except 1935–37 and 1972–75). About half the globe's current grandmasters are from the USSR, whose leading competitors are recognized as the best in the world. Chess in Russia is a national pastime, with columns appearing in practically all the newspapers and a run of a hundred thousand or more on a chess book selling out in a single day. The game is an integral part of the school curriculum, and the supremacy of Soviet teachers and trainers is undeniable—they have evolved the game to an almost pure science. Nowhere else on earth are chess professionals held in such high esteem or accorded such distinguished celebrity.

In *Russian Chess* I have focused on the younger generation of Russian players for the simple reason that they have become the center of the action. The famed older grandmasters are being displaced by the energetic vanguard. In a team match in Belgrade in 1970, the USSR pitched its top ten grandmasters against a group of ten opposing grandmasters representing the rest of the world. But for a similar London team event of 1984 from which the Russians also emerged victorious, only three of the Soviet players from 1970 made the team. A whole new crop of Russian players have stolen the limelight, and they will lord it over world-class chess for years to come.

What is so distinctive about these new Soviet contenders? Their styles are hard to characterize because they are so diverse. Generally, they exhibit a fiercely contentious will to win. They are magnificently creative when it comes to gaining the initiative. They are prodigiously resourceful in finding active defensive counterattacks (some of their top players are most dangerous when losing). Their games, moreover, can be seen as a careful and thorough study in openings, where myriad innovative tactics and unusual positional motifs abound. In this regard their key ploy is to maneuver for asymmetrical positions, where each combatant has different but offsetting advantages and liabilities—a ploy which really favors the better player. Above all, they are superb analysts who see profoundly into all positions.

How do these young lions differ from the older generation of Soviet grandmasters? Mainly they're better schooled than the greats: they learned from the best!

In this book, six grandmaster games—representing the spectrum of contemporary Russian chess—are laid out in six separate chapters. Each game is introduced with a discussion of its key themes under a heading called "What to Look For." Then comes the game with analysis of each move. What's unusual about this is the detailed format of asking an instructive question on every single play. The answer to each question is given both specifically and generally, which allows the timely introduction of concepts: principles, advice, rules, maxims, techniques, methods, and practical suggestions that hammer home or correlate the preceding discussion. Each concept really constitutes a cogent chess lesson in itself, and there are over a hundred of them in the book. Altogether they form a complete manual on how to radically improve your chess. Throughout, supplementing and reinforcing the procession of moves, questions, answers, and lessons, are illuminating quotes from top Russian players and thinkers. And summing up each chapter is a final postscript. The whole is an interactive learning experience that could only be compared to having a tireless chess master constantly at your side.

The games were selected to display the most complete range of ideas of Russian chess in integrated text. The six top grandmasters who contributed these games reflect the divergent styles of today's Soviet chess hegemony. It's regrettable that space does not permit the inclusion of games from other younger Russian grandmasters. These may be presented in another volume.

Russian Chess fuses the exciting world of Soviet chess with a revolutionary interactive format. It's a vital adjunct to mastering the game, whether your goal is to conquer the chess world or merely your next opponent.

ABOUT ALGEBRAIC NOTATION

The best way to read this book is while sitting at a chessboard on the White side, with the pieces in their starting positions. Most of the material can be understood without playing out the moves, by either reading the descriptive comments or examining the helpful diagrams accompanying the text. But you will derive greater benefit if you learn the simplified algebraic notation offered here. The system works as follows:

- The board is regarded as an eight-by-eight graph with sixty-four squares in all.
- The *files* (the rows of squares going up the board) are lettered a through h, beginning from White's left.
- The *ranks* (the rows of squares going across the board) are numbered 1 through 8, beginning from White's nearest row.
  You can therefore identify any square by combining a letter and a number, with the letter written first (see diagram A). For example, the square on which White's King stands in the original position is e1, while the original square for Black's King is e8. All squares are always named from White's point of view.

SYMBOLS YOU SHOULD KNOW

K means King
Q means Queen
R means Rook
B Means Bishop
N means Knight

Pawns are not symbolized when recording the moves. But if referred to in discussions, they are named by the letter of the file occupied—the pawn on the b-file is the b-pawn. If a pawn makes a capture, one merely indicates the file the capturing pawn starts on. Thus, if a White pawn on b2 captures a Black pawn, Knight, Bishop, Rook or Queen on a3, it is written **bxa3**. In indicating a capture, name the square captured, not the enemy unit.

x means captures
+ means check
0-0 means castles Kingside
0-0-0 means castles Queenside
! means good move
!! means very good move
? means questionable move
?? means blunder
?! means risky move but worth considering
!? means probably a good move but unclear
1. means White's first move
1... means Black's first move (when appearing independently of White's)
(1–0) means White wins
(0–1) means Black wins

READING THE LINE SCORE OF A GAME

Consider diagram B. White could mate in three moves and it would be written this way:

1. Nc7 + Kb8 2. Na6 + Ka8 3. Bc6 mate.
1. Nc7 + means that White's first move was Knight moves to c7 giving check.
   Kb8 means that Black's first move was King to b8.
2. Na6 + means that White's second move was Knight to a6 check.
   Ka8 means that Black's second move was King to a8.
3. Bc6 mate means that White's third move was Bishop to c6 giving mate.

Note that the number of the move is written only once, appearing just before White's play. In this book, the actual moves are given in **boldface** type. The analyzed alternatives appear in regular type.

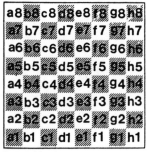

DIAGRAM A

DIAGRAM B

THE PLAYERS

Don't forget to refer to the Grandmaster Glossary in the back for brief biographies of all the chess players featured in this book.

RUSSIAN

CHESS

LESSON 1

Light Squares, Time, and Attack

WHITE: Cernin
BLACK: Miles
Tunis 1985

WHAT TO LOOK FOR

This game is unusual in that both White and Black try to implement the same ideas, but White's more timely moves work against Black's poor preparation. Both players offer a gambit, both bring out their Queens early, and neither castles. Miles, a powerful grandmaster from England, is bold and innovative. But in this instance, his sharp attempts are rebuffed by a sound, concisely mustered counterattack.

> **KORCHNOI:** I like to coax my opponents into attacking, to let them taste the joy of the initiative, so that they may get carried away, become careless, and sacrifice material.

GAMBIT PLAY

A gambit is a voluntary sacrifice in the opening. Usually one gambits a pawn to gain an attack, increase the initiative, or to obtain a lead in development. Early pawn gambits make sense because pawns are less valuable in the opening than they are later, in the endgame. In openings it's more important to build a strong attack and to direct the flow of play. In theory, if you can win in the opening by sacrificing a pawn, you needn't worry about being behind a pawn in the endgame; the game will never last that long.

BOTVINNIK: It is peculiar, but a fact nevertheless, that gamblers in chess always have enthusiastic followers.

But your sacrifice might result in no significant advantage in time or attack and the defender may eventually consolidate, with an extra pawn to boot. So gambits can be quite risky, and tradition-minded players generally don't make them. No such restrictions exist in the Russian school, where players pull out rabbits for whatever the position calls for. Depending on circumstances, they are equally willing to defend against gambits or offer them. Certainly, the demands on the gambiteer are great.

KOBLENTZ: The attacker must have a lasting initiative in hand, and must be able to conjure up constant threats to the opposing King. This enables him to dictate the attacking tempo, to force his will upon his opponent, and thereby impede or prevent enemy freeing maneuvers.

COLOR PLAY

In many games, each competitor establishes his play on squares of a particular color. He positions his pieces and pawns so that they control squares of the same color, and also tries to dispel or drive away enemy units that influence these squares. One thus may play a *light-square game* or a *dark-square game*. Such control often hinges on the placement of a fianchettoed (flanked) Bishop which, poised on the wing but directed at the center, controls a diagonal of squares of the same color.

White opens up with **1. d4.**

Q: *What are the basic aims of this strong opening thrust?*

It immediately lays claim to a key central square, e5, while also attacking the important point c5. The move clears the dark-square Bishop's diagonal as well as providing the Queen with some scope along the expanding d-file. If opportune, White will follow shortly with e4, creating a classic pawn center.

Black should try to stop or discourage White from doing this, or allow White to create a pawn center and then attempt to undermine it, a popular contemporary approach. Formerly, attacking players preferred beginning with 1. e4 and positional players began with 1. d4, because of its slower nature and greater opportunity for maneuvering. Many top young Russians are currently honing 1. d4 systems into sharp attacking weapons, defying the traditional logic.

KERES: In our time, almost every master makes a thorough study of opening schemes that are popular and often used in modern tournaments. These variations are often prolonged deep into the middlegame, with almost every possibility already analyzed at home. This way players have little to create over the board, they just repeat home analysis . . . It would be a pity if, in modern tournaments, the game of chess actually began with the middlegame.

BOTVINNIK: The opening is important if it is an introduction to a scene called "the middlegame." It is of little help in winning the game if the middlegame plan is only weakly linked to the opening.

Top Russian grandmasters are opinionated and often at loggerheads. They have a dynamic approach to chess, depicted in their willingness to defend either side of a balanced position.

Black answers 1 . . . **Nf6.**

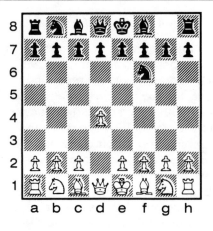

Q: What is Black's defensive plan?

Superficially, Black's developing move stops 2. e4, and the establishment of an ominous White center. An older, more direct effort to stop White's e-pawn from going two squares is 1 . . . d5, creating a double Queen-pawn defense. While 1 . . . Nf6 is not really better than 1 . . . d5, it's more flexible, for it doesn't commit the Black pawn structure to a definite formation, as 1 . . . d5 clearly does. Black is less declarative in playing **1 . . . Nf6,** because whatever defense Black ultimately chooses, he probably would develop his Knight to f6 anyway. But he might not place his pawn on d5 (rather on d6).

So the early d-pawn movement gives away more of his intentions than the immediate development of the King-Knight. Another point: White is still uncertain how Black means to develop his King-Bishop. Will he transport it through the center by moving the e-pawn, or will he post it flankwise by playing a subsequent g6? Black's poker-faced **1 . . . Nf6** is the most plausible first move answer to 1. d4.

White continues **2. Nf3.**

Q: Is this the most usual move here?

No. More frequent is 2. c4, augmenting White's space on the Queenside and his Queen's access there. The pawn on c4 pressures d5 and increases chances of an exchange of pawns to open the c-file. White's **2. Nf3** is also somewhat noncommittal, however, for he would probably develop his Knight to this square regardless. White too could flank his King-Bishop or engage it through the center after moving his e-pawn.

Black plays **2 . . . e6.**

Q: What does this reveal about Black's King-Bishop development?

Mostly that Black will not flank his King-Bishop, developing it rather along the a3-f8 diagonal. The Bishop will not likely be flanked now, for that entails moving the g-pawn. Black would then have moved two pawns (the g-pawn and the e-pawn), one unnecessarily. Moving only one pawn will let out the King-Bishop, so the advance g6 would then be wasted. Moreover, after both e6 and g6, the dark squares on Black's Kingside would be weakened, especially f6, which could never again be guarded by a Black pawn. White might be able to operate on those squares without being forced into retreat by the defending pawns. So **2 . . . e6** commits Black to a candid, nonflanking development of his King-Bishop.

White answers **3. c4.**

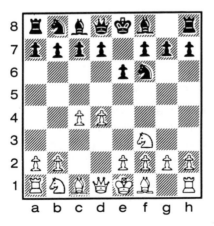

Q: What does this sortie accomplish?

As indicated earlier, it's quite useful. It gives White more space for Rooks and the Queen behind the advancing pawn. White's Queen perhaps could station itself at a4, b3, or c2. At a4 it pecks away at the Queenside, at b3 it assails b7 and d5, and at c2 it surveys the c-file and the square e4, supporting the King-pawn's movement. And **3. c4** also reinforces the future advance d5, amplifying White's space and cramping Black.

CONCEPT: In most Queen-pawn openings, neither player wants to block his c-pawn with a Knight. Usually it's better to first move the c-pawn before developing the Knight to c3. Moving the c-pawn opens lines, increases space, and enhances central attacking possibilities.

Q: How can you tell if you have a spatial advantage?

There are two ways to determine this. In open games, where pieces can freely move through the center, you probably have a spatial edge if your pieces occupy and guard more squares in your opponent's half of the board than his pieces do in yours— that is, if you control a greater portion of the board. In closed games, where the center is blocked by impeding pawns, you tend to have more space if your pawns are further advanced. This gives you somewhat more room behind the lines, and your pieces can reposition and maneuver with greater ease than your opponent's.

Black responds with **3 . . . c5.**

Q: Why this move?

Black envisions an exchange of his c-pawn for White's d-pawn, thus obtaining an advantage of two center pawns to one. With more pawns in the center, you probably have a better chance to control the middle board and the direction of the game. Second, Black also develops Queenside counterplay while opening lines for his pieces, as White did with the move **3. c4.**

CONCEPT: Try to gain a central majority of pawns by exchanging c- and f-pawns for d- and e-pawns respectively.

White forges ahead with **4. d5.**

Q: *Doesn't this advance waste time, in moving something that's already been moved? Shouldn't White use this tempo to develop another piece?*

Every action you make in chess requires a weighing of what you get against what you give up. White must expend another tempo to move the d-pawn, but how else is he to avert its exchange for Black's c-pawn? And though White loses a little time, more valuably he gains space. His pawn at d5 will severely cramp Black, more than balancing the extra tempo needed to get the pawn to the 5th rank. You can't get something for nothing in chess. You must give to get.

CONCEPT: Be prepared to exchange one type of advantage for another (for example, space for time) if it improves your overall position.

Black sallies **4 . . . b5.**

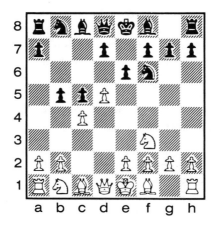

Q: Can't White now win a pawn?

If White were reckless enough to pilfer a pawn by the forcible 5. cxb5, it would leave his own d-pawn vulnerable to capture. He could instead play 5. dxe6, and after 5 . . . fxe6 (capturing toward the center to increase the number of pawns there and gain control of that region), White emerges a pawn ahead (by 6. cxb5). But this doesn't really win him anything. He has merely accepted the gambit pawn Black has offered, with some sticky strings attached.

After a subsequent . . . d5, Black will hold ultimate sway in the center and substantial attacking possibilities. Havoc threatens from Bishops posted at b7 and d6, which are aimed at the White Kingside behind a central armada of pawns. Moreover, the connected central pawns Black gets will have enormous potential to expand, clearing out a great deal of territory. So White, if accepting the gambit, would have to blunt the Black attack and arrive at an endgame a pawn to the good. Black offers the pawn believing he can break through decisively long before the endgame. Whoever plays better will probably win.

The great crucible of most contemporary openings is the fight for the initiative. Whoever can seize and maintain it possesses the overriding superiority in a chess position. The Soviet school, now led by a brilliant young coterie of commando-type players, has infused the initial phase of the game with extreme tension, in which the slightest distraction is fatal. Let your guard down for an instant and the entire game can turn irreversibly against you.

White ignores Black's gambit and plays **5. Bg5.**

ALEKHINE: On principle, in the opening I never try to obtain such an advantage. It can only be had at the cost of time and development, which often proves fatal.

Q: What does White gain by refusing the gambit?

For one, White gains in development, by pinning the Knight

that attacks the central squares d5 and e4. And White maintains his beachhead—the staunch pawn at d5—which still cramps Black's game. Ignoring the gambit offer also means that Black has wasted a tempo, for **4 . . . b5** contributes nothing developmentally meaningful. White has opted to keep his central pawns rather than abandon the area for an unclear material advantage.

Black attacks White's Bishop by **5 . . . h6.**

Q: *Doesn't this move waste time?*

It may seem to, for the h6 push really adds nothing to development. In fact, the advance slightly weakens the g6 square, since the h-pawn no longer guards it. Such attacks by Rook-pawns on Bishops that pin Knights are categorized as "putting the question to the Bishop"—Will the Bishop capture the pinned Knight or retreat?

If the Bishop retreats to h4, for example, Black has the option of breaking the pin by playing g5, compelling the Bishop to move again and freeing the Knight. The drawback to a g5-type advance is that it generally loosens Black's pawn structure. Just imagine the potential destruction White's pieces can wreak on the Kingside.

If White captures the Knight instead (Bxf6), Black winds up developing his Queen to f6, which may be good or bad. Though it develops a new piece, bringing the Queen out prematurely exposes it to enemy attack. In addition to the Black Kingside weaknesses, the other irrevocable factor is that White exchanges a Bishop for a Knight, which in the opening of an unsettled game may be imprudent. In most positions Bishops tend to dominate Knights. The exception is locked games, where Bishops are obstructed by pawns that Knights can jump over. A further consequence of the exchange of Bishop for Knight is the weakening of White's dark squares. This could be significant later on.

CONCEPT: If the opening is unclear, avoid exchanging Bishops for Knights, unless the position definitely requires your doing so.

Q: Can Black win a pawn by 5 . . . bxc4?

Perhaps. He goes up a pawn right away, but loses time in the process. Anyway, there's really no way to maintain the pawn if White should go after it. White can count on a powerful game by continuing with moves like Nc3, e4, Bxc4, and/or Nd2-c4. Pawns like this Black doesn't need.

White exchanges Bishop for Knight **6. Bxf6.**

Q: What advantage comes to White by this exchange?

White gains a move and thereby retains the initiative. If White had retreated his Bishop, Black could freely continue with his own plans. But since Black must recapture the Bishop to maintain material equality, it's White who obtains freedom of choice. The exchange also strengthens White in the center, for he removes an important protector of e4 and d5.

CONCEPT: Sometimes you can gain a move by exchanging pieces. But what does this really gain if in exchanging you develop your opponent's game usefully?

Black takes the Bishop back with his Queen **6 . . . Qxf6.**

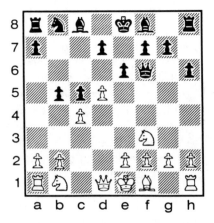

Q: *Would it have been better to take back with the pawn?*

It would have been worse. Black does get more pawns in the center and an open g-file after 6 . . . gxf6, but the overall damage to his Kingside pawn structure means that his King lacks safe haven there. Since his Queenside is already exposed, Black's King must cling to the center, exposed to possible heavy artillery. Taking back with the Queen on f6 also contains a surface threat to White's b-pawn that should be answered.

CONCEPT: Try to avoid doubling your pawns unless you have no choice or can gain a clearly greater advantage in the resulting attack or through the opening of lines.

White protects his b-pawn by **7. Qc2.**

Q: *What else does 7. Qc2 do besides protect the b-pawn?*

At c2, White's Queen is quite functionally placed. It's main duties are to guard over e4, supporting the eventual advance of White's King-pawn. Additionally, the Queen from c2 protects c4, now being assailed. Compare the early development of Queens. White's sits safe and powerful on the second rank, while Black's remains a potential target for White's marching pawns and nimble pieces, as we'll soon see.

Black captures White's d-pawn **7 . . . exd5.**

Q: *Would it make more sense to capture White's c-pawn (7 . . . bxc4), forcing White's Queen to move again?*

No, for White does not intend playing 8. Qxc4. Instead he wants to develop 8. Nc3 (followed by 9. e4 and 10. Bxc4). Black cannot afford to waste any more time on feckless pawn moves, trying to hold onto his ill-gotten pawn. Also, such a capture defies the purpose of Black's initial gambit: to sacrifice to build a classic pawn center. Since White hasn't bitten, Black must consider changing his plans.

White takes back the pawn **8. cxd5.**

Q: What about the deployment of pawns and future plans of attack?

Superficially, White's chances now lie in the center, with more pawns than his opponent has on the two central files. Black's attack should come on the Queenside, where he has the advantage of three pawns to two. In terms of pawn majorities, you have a majority if, over any number of consecutive files, your pawns exceed your opponent's.

If each side has a different majority, then the pawn structure is *unbalanced* or *asymmetrical*. *Balanced pawn structures* are those in which each side has the same number of pawns on their corresponding files. It's generally harder to outplay your opponent in balanced, symmetrical games, which explains why the young Russians are so keen on creating disparate setups right at the beginning.

CONCEPT: Direct your attack from your greatest concentration of forces, especially pawns. Look for favorable asymmetry.

Black secures his center with **8 . . . d6.**

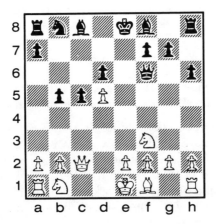

Q: *How does this counter White's central plans?*

Black sees that White intends advance of his e-pawn to e4 and, if feasible, to e5. By controlling e5 from d6, Black dissuades White from this strategy before making further preparation.

White continues **9. e4.**

Q: *Is White threatening anything?*

Black's b-pawn is now up for grabs, since White can take it incisively and with check by 10. Bxb5 + . Black could defend it with 9 . . . b4, though that would weaken the light squares on the Queenside. In particular, Black would be jettisoning square c4, which could be beautifully occupied by White after Nb-d2 and Nc4. Also bad is 9 . . . c4, for in a few moves, White could undermine the entire Black pawn edifice on the Queenside.

CONCEPT: Don't carelessly make premature and unsupported early pawn moves. They can lead to irreparable damage, for pawns, unlike pieces, can't move backward.

PETROSIAN: How often has it been repeated that pawn moves must be considered with discretion?

Black upholds his pawn by **9 . . . a6.**

Q: *How can White weaken Black's Queenside?*

To do so, he must induce the Black pawns to move and relinquish control over certain squares, making them more vulnerable to attack in being closer to White's forces and further away from his own. How to do this will soon be made clear.

CONCEPT: To weaken your opponent's pawns, force them to move.

White lashes out with **10. a4.**

Q: Would either 10 . . . Bd7 or 10 . . . bxa4 be an effective counter?

The defensive 10 . . . Bd7 loses a pawn, for White plays 11.axb5, when Black is unable to capture back on b5 safely because of the pin along the a-file, from White's Rook to Black's. Capturing White's pawn with 10 . . . bxa4 is admittedly better but subjects Black to other problems: the resultant weak squares on the Queenside (mainly a6 and c4, the light squares).

Black gives in and pushes his pawn **10 . . . b4.**

Q: How does this insure White's domination of the light squares on the Queenside?

White now holds sway over the Queenside light squares for two reasons: the f1-a6 diagonal is open for White's Bishop, and Black has no means to stop White from occupying c4 with a Knight. These two strengths accrue to White after the advance of Black's b-pawn.

White maneuvers his Knight **11. Nb-d2.**

Q: Where is this Knight headed, and why?

It's going to c4, where it majestically overlooks the central squares e5 and d6 and supports the timely advance of White's e-pawn. When that break occurs, White should come away with at least a dangerous passed d-pawn and mean attacking chances via the opening of the middle lines.

Black brings out his Queen-Bishop **11 . . . Bg4.**

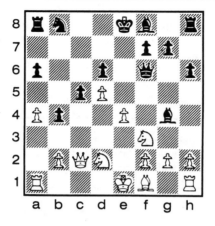

Q: Does this counter White's plans?

It certainly stops the immediate 12. Nc4, for 12 . . . Bxf3 13. gxf3 Qxf3 brightens Black's game. But considering the backward nature of Black's development and disharmonious configuration, 12 . . . Nd7 would have been wiser. This nicely copes with his opponent's upcoming resource, as White's next move reveals. Black's Bishop development is simply premature.

White sacrifices a pawn **12. e5!**

Q: Why does White give away this pawn?

Black originally offered White a gambit on the 4th move with the advance b5. White declined and now offers his own, instantly infusing life into the arena. White could easily have quietly continued his development by 12. Be2, and after 12 . . . Nd7, proffered a trade by 13. Ng1, when 13 . . . Bxe2 14. Nxe2 gives White a small but definite edge. But with this sacrifice, which cannot profitably be declined, White has multipurpose aims.

After **12. e5!** he gains:

- A passed d-pawn.
- The central square e4, especially for his Knight.
- Harassment of Black's Queen.
- An open diagonal for his Queen and Bishop (from d3).

KOTOV: Soviet masters are constantly finding new possibilities in the opening as they strive to introduce elements of a tense, acute struggle, beginning with the earliest moves.

Black captures the White pawn **12 . . . dxe5.**

Q: Can't Black retreat his Queen to e7, pinning the e-pawn?

This withdrawal fails to the punishing 13. Ne4. Some of the possibilities are:

A) 13 . . . dxe5 14. d6 Qe6 (on 14 . . . Qd7 White has the simple 15. Nxe5) 15. Bc4 is strong for White.

B) 13 . . . Bxf3 14. Nxd6+ Kd8 (14 . . . Kd7 is answered with the same move) 15. Qf5, threatening 16. Qc8 mate.

White forges ahead with **13. Ne4.**

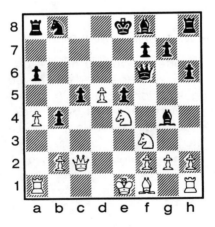

Q: *How do the two Queens now stand?*

Both Queens moved early. But whereas White's was invulnerable, Black's is under fire and endangered. To extricate Her Majesty, Black must sacrifice more time.

CONCEPT: If your opponent brings out his Queen early, try to gain time, attacking it while developing and improving the position of your pieces.

Black flees by **13 . . . Qf4.**

Q: *Are either 13 . . . Qe7 or 13 . . . Qf5 better for Black?*

As in the previous discussion, 13 . . . Qe7 leads to 14. d6 Qe6 15. Bc4, with advantage to White. And 13 . . . Qf5 runs smack into 14. Bd3 and the menaced discovery 15. Nd6 +, winning Black's Queen. Black now starts to pay the piper for this dubious Queen development.

White repositioned his King-Knight **14. Nf-d2!.**

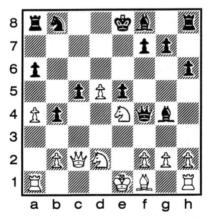

Q: *What reasons compelled this maneuver?*

It secures both Knights. White's central pirouetter at e4 is now guarded twice, and his Kingside Knight is no longer under attack. White meanwhile gets a greater grip on the light squares as he prepares to occupy c4, with tremendous pressure against Black's position.

CONCEPT: Before occupying certain squares, it helps to have total control of them, so that pieces placed there can't be driven away.

Black attacks him **14 . . . Bf5.**

Q: *What does Black intend?*

One reason for this pin is to prevent 15. Nxc5, which would win a pawn. But Black mainly is defending against an insidious threat. White has planned to attack Black's Queen by 15. g3. For example, after the natural 14 . . . Nd7, developing a new piece, White plays 15.g3 and Black responds with the forced 15 . . . Qf5. White then wins a piece by 16. h3, for if 16 . . . Bf3, then 17. Nd6+ discovers a winning attack to Black's Queen from White's. After 17. Nd6+ Bxd6 18. Qxf5 Bxh1 19. Nc4, White's Old Man River game simply rolls along. He will follow with natural moves such as castling Queenside, developing his Bishop to h3, and possibly capturing on h1.

By playing **14 . . . Bf5,** Black can answer 15. g3 with 15 . . . Bxe4, when 16. Nxe4 allows 16 . . . Qf3, and at least temporary relief for the Queen. The best move for Black may be 14 . . . h5, providing his Queen with the useful retreat Qh6. But this is by no means an obvious defense, and itself is quite sharp.

CONCEPT: When your opponent makes an obvious threat (such as 15. Nxc5), it may be combined with a hidden threat that you might miss because your attention is too much focused on the obvious or direct attack. Conversely, set up double attacks, especially those that combine candid threats with subtle ones. The brutish ones may disguise deadlier, undetected possibilities.

White builds his game by **15. Bd3.**

Q: Does 15 . . . Nd7 now give Black good defensive chances?

To evaluate 15 . . . Nd7, we should consider the forcing line beginning with 16. g3. After 16 . . . Qg4 17. d6 (to restrict Black's King-Bishop and to unveil the a2-f7 diagonal) 17 . . . Qg6 18. 0-0, White has a strong attack and a significant advantage in space. Here, 18 . . . Bxd6 fails to 19. Nxd6+ Qxd6 20. Bxf5. Less playable for Black in this variation would be 17 . . . Bxe4 (instead of 17 . . . Qg6). After 18. Nxe4 f5 19. Nxc5 Qf3 20. 0-0 Rc8 21. Bxf5, Black's game soon disintegrates. If 21 . . . Rxc5, 22. Bxd7+ wins the Rook; and if 21 . . . Nxc5, then 22. Bxc8 conquers the Rook a different way. But White could misstep too. After 15 . . . Nd7 16. g3 Qg4, rash would be 17. Nd6+?, when 17 . . . Bxd6 18. Bxf5 Qg5 19. Ne4 Qe7 is unclear.

CONCEPT: If you have the advantage, you may have to nurse it along with a reasonable amount of preparation. Don't throw it all away by striking out brusquely with showy tactics that are less effective than safer, less flashy moves. The Russian school appreciates the fine balance between attack and preparation.

> **ESTRIN: A constant reevaluation of values is taking place.**

Black takes White's Knight **15 . . . Bxe4.**

Q: Should White now recapture with his Bishop?

The problem with 16. Bxe4 is that it could give Black time to consolidate. He might be able to play 16 . . . Bd6, and if 17. Nc4, hold the fort by 17 . . . Qf6.

White takes back **16. Nxe4.**

Q: How would you describe White's Knight at e4?

The Knight is powerfully posted on e4, overlooking important squares in Black's terrain.

Black safeguards with **16 . . . Nd7.**

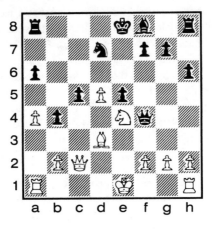

Q: Can White now play 17. d6?

After 17. d6, Black could lash out with 17 . . . f5, when
18.Nxc5 runs into the complications of 18 . . . e4. And if 19.
Nxd7, then exd3 seems to keep the shoelaces tied.

White attacks the Queen **17. g3.**

Q: How should White answer 17 . . . Qf5 and 17 . . . Qf3?

On 17 . . . Qf5, White wins the Queen by the discovery, 18.
Nd6+. On 17 . . . Qf3, White can castle! This highlights a
major difference in the two positions. Neither side has yet
castled, and neither does. But White always retains the option
of doing so, and doesn't because he always has something
better to do—White's King is never in real danger. On the other
hand, Black doesn't castle simply because he never gets the

chance. Deprived of respite in defending against White's numerous threats, he never has time to get his King to safety.

CONCEPT: Castle early if it improves your position or serves some definite purpose. But don't just automatically castle, especially if there are more immediate or pressing concerns. On the other hand, make sure you have the option of castling quickly, in case you suddenly have to.

Black moves **17 . . . Qg4.**

Q: Can White advance 18. d6 now?

Again, the counterthrust 18 . . . f5 seems to inject Black with enough life for White not to play 18. d6. An advantage must be milked before it produces any cheese.

White continues **18. h3.**

Q: How does Black fare after 18 . . . Qg6, 18 . . . Qf5, and 18 . . . Qf3 respectively?

After 18 . . . Qg6, White wins a pawn by 19. Nxc5. After 18 . . . Qf5, White wins the Queen by 19. Nd6 +, uncloseting an attack to the enemy Queen. And after 18 . . . Qf3, the game might go 19. 0-0, and if 19 . . . f5, then 20. Nd2 snares the f-pawn and penetrates the Black bastions.

Black retorts **18 . . . Qh5.**

Q: Why not the immediate 19. g4?

This unnecessarily drains blood from the square h4, which can now be used by the Black Queen to recuperate from White's harassment. White's next move proves most timely.

White finally plays **19. d6!.**

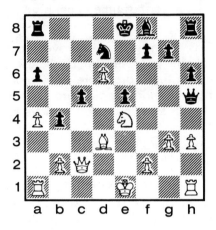

Q: Doesn't Black win the d-pawn here, driving away White's Knight by 19 . . . f5?

This thrust is past its prime. After 19 . . . f5 20. Nxc5 e4, White can gain a vital tempo with 21. Be2, retaining numerous threats. Black could instead answer 20. Nxc5 with 20 . . . Rc8, but that fails to 21. Bxf5, and Black is up the creek. Black could try to first defend his c-pawn by 19 . . . Rc8, but that drops the a-pawn outright to 20. Bxa6.

Black stoically plays **19 . . . Qg6.**

Q: Can't White directly win the c-pawn?

The move 20. Nxc5 relieves the pressure on Black's game and allows 20 . . . Qxd6. Black might then be able to crawl back into the contest.

White indirectly protects his d-pawn with **20. Rd1.**

Q: *How does this save the d-pawn?*

After 20 . . . Bxd6 21. Nxd6+ Qxd6 22. Bb5 White wins the Knight and anything else he can. Notice White's growing dominance on the light squares.

Black counterattacks with **20 . . . b3.**

Q: *Why does Black offer this pawn?*

He hopes to divert White from his attack and to gain some counterplay himself. For example, after 21. Qxb3, Black might obtain some counteractivity along the b-file after 21 . . . Rb8.

CONCEPT: To break your opponent's attack, you may have to surrender some material. If on the attack, be leery of accepting pawn sacrifices that defuse your assault. The initiative you give up may be more important than the material you take.

White ignores the pawn and plays **21. Qe2.**

Q: *How does the Queen's repositioning help White's game?*

By not taking the pawn at b3, White keeps the b-file closed so that Black's Rook can't use it. At e2, the Queen strengthens her grip on key light squares, such as e4 and the e2-a6 and e2-h5 diagonals. Moreover, White creates possible, but veiled, threats along the e-file.

Black uppercuts with **21 . . . f5.**

Q: *Is White's Knight temporarily immune from capture?*

Apparently. If Black does play 22 . . . fxe4, then 23. Bxe4 forks Black's Queen and Rook at a8, getting for White more than enough material compensation for his lost Knight.

White surprises with **22. g4.**

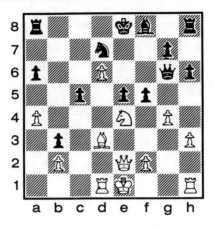

Q: Since Black clearly cannot take White's Knight, what is the purpose of 22. g4?

White is playing a light-square game. In fighting for control of the light squares, he wants to eliminate those Black pawns that can guard the light squares, particularly around the center. The advance **22. g4** seems to do this.

Black fights on with **22 . . . c4.**

Q: Why can't White capture the c-pawn with his Bishop?

If White captures 23. Bxc4, Black can remove the Knight at e4 without having to worry about a subsequent Bxe4, the Bishop no longer occupying the crucial diagonal.

White retains his grip with **23. Bb1.**

Q: Does White now threaten to capture the c-pawn with his Queen?

Yes, because his Knight would still be safe from seizure, in that 23 . . . fxe4 24. Bxe4 smacks of treacherous consequences.

Black takes White's g-pawn **23 . . . fxg4.**

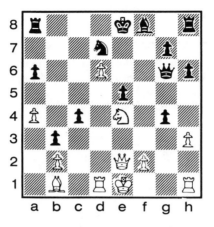

Q: Should White recapture his g-pawn with his Queen or pawn?

Neither one. Rather than taking the g-pawn, greater menace comes from the potent 24. Qxc4, which disarrays Black's game.

White plays **24. Qxc4.**

Q: Should Black continue with 24 . . . gxh3?

That loses to 25. Nc5, when 25 . . . Qg2 is met by the devastating 26. Be4.

Black defends by **24 . . . Qf7.**

Q: Should White trade Queens?

Trading Queens would be incorrect here, because after 25.Qxf7+ Kxf7 26. hxg4, Black would have some chances to organize a defense. By keeping the Queens on the board, White has the real possibility of developing a mating attack or of winning ample material.

CONCEPT: Avoid exchanges when attacking, unless they lead to a clear improvement of position. Indiscriminate trading will dissipate an attack.

KOBLENTZ: As a rule the attacker has well-placed pieces. He enjoys greater freedom of space. He can rapidly undermine strategic strongpoints, and thus he is able to pursue a variety of secondary objectives in addition to the ultimate aim.

White maintains the pressure with **25.Qc6.**

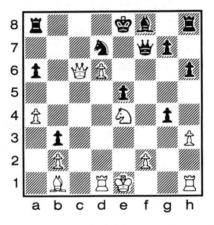

Q: How will White proceed?

By pinning the Knight at d7, White undoubtedly will consider intensifying that pressure, possibly with 26. Nc5. If Black plays unguardedly, say 25 . . . Rb8 and 26 . . . gxh3, White may have the opportunity for 27. Bg6, placing the Queen in a ruinous pin. If Black captures the Bishop 27 . . . Qxg6, then 28. Qxd7 is mate. Black's next move saves the Rook and deals with this problem by strengthening his Knight.

Black guards his Knight with **25 . . . Rd8.**

Q: Should White take the a-pawn with his Queen?

After 26. Qxa6, Black has some slight counterplay in 26 . . . gxh3 or even 26 . . . Qf3 first. White must avoid unnecessary complications and quell any Black uprisings.

White quietly takes back the g-pawn **26. hxg4.**

ALEKHINE: The strongest continuation of the attack, and at the same time, setting a trap.

Q: Does Black now have the resource 26 . . . Qf3?

White has a number of reasonable answers to this invasion, centering around moving his Knight. After 27. Ng5, for example, Black gets mated if he takes White's Queen by 28. Bg6! He could defend, however, with 27 . . . Qf6, guarding g6. But White could first play 27. Rg1, and follow with 28. Nc5, among other possibilities.

Black plays **26 . . . g6.**

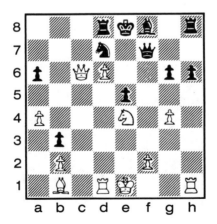

Q: What is Black's aim here?

He still hopes to complete his Kingside development by 27 . . . Bg7 and then he wants to castle, removing his King from the center and considerably lessening the pressure on his position.

White forges ahead with **27. Nc5.**

Q: What are some of White's potential threats?

White may be able to capture on a6, creating a clear path for his own a-pawn. Or he can try to shift the Rooks into the game along the third rank, over to the f-file. Or he can relocate the Bishop at e4, where it menaces the square d5. These possibilities loom large.

Black inches over with **27 . . . Rg8.**

Q: What's intended with this move?

Probably to strengthen g6, thus freeing the Queen for duty elsewhere. Before 27 . . . Rg8, the Queen was chained to the defense of g6, eyed by White's nauseating Bishop.

White centralizes his Bishop **28. Be4.**

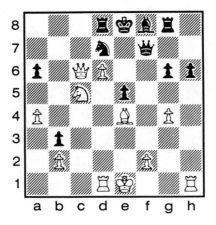

> **GREKOV:** At a time when all of White's pieces are in play, Black's King is not even castled and his King-Bishop is still on its home square. Retribution is not long deferred.

Q: What's the threat?

To the naked eye, the threat is 29. Bd5, skewering the Queen and Rook. Also plausible is the capture on a6 with the Knight, threatening 30. Nc7 mate. Black's future looks bleak.

Black develops his Bishop **28 . . . Bg7.**

Q: Doesn't this lose the exchange, at least a Rook for a Bishop?

At least that, but Black must realize that his game is gone and is merely plodding along. White can win in any number of ways.

White usurps the a-pawn **29. Nxa6.**

Q: Now what is White threatening?

Depending on the proper order and how Black now responds, White can choose from Bd5, Nc7+ and Ne6+, Qc4, Rh3, Rd3, and so on. This game is gone with the wind.

Black clears a square for his King with **29 . . . Qf4.**

Q. Is Black really threatening the g-pawn?

It's an empty, meaningless attack. White's threats are more serious and the game is all but filed away. Black's inertia in a lost cause is a subject for wonder.

White checks the King **30.Nc7 +.**

Q: *Where should Black move his King—to f8 or f7?*

Zounds! Does it really matter? Moving it to f8 loses the Queen to the Knight fork 31. Ne6 +. Moving it to f7 loses the Queen in a similar way, as the game shows.

Black flees by **30 . . . Kf7.**

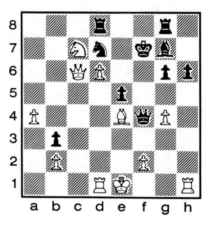

Q: *Should White now play 31. Bd5 + ?*

No, unless he doesn't want to win Black's Queen. While 31.Bd5 + skewers the King and Rook, it blocks the square d5, which is needed by White's Knight.

White pursues the attack with **31. Qc4 + .**

Q: *Is there any way to avoid the loss of Black's Queen?*

Not now. If 31 . . . Kf8, 32. Ne6 + forks the two big pieces. And on 31 . . . Kf6, White has 32. Nd5 + .

Black doggedly continues **31 . . . Kf6.**

Q: *Why doesn't Black resign?*

He's either waiting for a miracle or Godot.

White wins the Queen with **32. Nd5 +**.
BLACK RESIGNS.

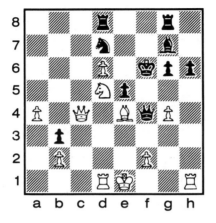

POSTSCRIPT

White conducted the attack beautifully, never losing control of the game. Black offered a gambit, White turned it down for development. When White offered a gambit, it had to be accepted, which led to increase in his initiative. Both Kings remained in the center, but White kept his there by choice. Black never got the chance to castle. If there was one overriding characteristic of White's attack, it was the play on the light squares. Consider the thrust of his actions:

   A) The removal of Black pieces that guarded light squares.
   • The capture of the Knight on f6 **(6. Bxf6)**.
   • Forcing Black to capture the Knight on e4 with his light-square Bishop **(15 . . . Bxe4)**.

   B) The use of White's pawns to gain light-square control.
   • **10. a4.**
   • **22. g4!.**
   • The clearance sacrifice **12. e5!**, so the Knight could occupy e4.

C) The use of light squares by White pieces.
- **7. Qc2.**
- **13. Ne4.**
- The possibility of Nc4.
- **21. Qe2.**
- **25. Qc6.**
- The possibility of Bxf5.
- **28. Be4.**
- The possibility of Bd5.
- **32. Nd5+.**

White displayed a very mature game—the right blend of attack and preparation, at the right times.

Open Lines, the Center, and the Uncastled King

WHITE: Miles
BLACK: Belyavsky
Wijk ann Zee 1984

WHAT TO LOOK FOR

This contest is a total and unending fight for the initiative, with material sacrificed at key points so that Black can stay a move on top of the attack. White never really gets the opportunity to organize his forces, finally succumbing to furious warfare waged across the entire board.

> VAINSTEIN: The philosophy of chess is the philosophy of a sharp, logical conflict, resolved by explosive means.

PLAY IN THE CENTER

Both players jockey for control of this sector with their pawns, trying to guard the central squares and using other pawns as bait to establish dominance in the middle. White's exertion of maximum pressure coerces Black into abandoning his occupation of the center. The resulting open lines, however, wind up favoring Black, who with better development, is prepared to utilize them.

GAMBIT PLAY

As in Lesson 1, some of the fight spins around gambited pawns—whether to take or not. If you can get away with capturing them, surely do so. But if their capture is time-consuming, it could be prudent not to take them. Here the gambits are offered to gain time and open lines for attack, and it's Black who makes them work.

ATTACKING THE KING IN THE CENTER

White's King gets trapped in the center, and he never can garner the time to extricate it. The attack builds slowly. Initially the sacrifices are light, but as the assault force grows, Black can offer more and more to prevent White from consolidating and castling. Finally, the White Queen is lured away. With all of Black's pieces participating, White's end comes suddenly, though not unexpectedly.

THE PIN

A pin is a *tactic* (a short-range operation, which is specific and direct, as opposed to strategy, which is long-term and general) by which a Queen, Rook, or Bishop attacks two enemy men along the same line (rank, file, or diagonal), so that moving the first man exposes the second man to capture. In this game, Black takes advantage of a pin to fuel his attack. White takes only halfway measures to deal with it, rather than coping with it immediately. The results for White are regrettable.

CONCEPT: Try to set up pins. After doing so, see if you can apply more pressure to the pinned enemy man. If unable to move, it may not be able to save itself.

White begins with **1. c4.**

Q: What's good about this move?

Since the c-pawn is not a center pawn, its movement doesn't release as many pieces as does moving the d- or e-pawn. The advance permits only White's Queen to enter the fray, which in most openings is the piece to be developed least. The advance does strike at a central square (d5), however, and it's so flexible that a number of plans may be suitable to it.

The opener **1. c4** is known as the English Opening, supposedly named for Howard Staunton (1810-74), the self-proclaimed British World Champion of the 1850s. It's an opening with tremendous transpositional possibilities—by playing the next few moves in varied sequences, different openings can result. It could remain an English Opening, or become a Reti (1.Nf3 d5 2. c4), a Queen's Gambit (1. d4 d5 2. c4), or any of the Indian systems.

> **BRONSTEIN:** The openings merely have different names—the strategy in them can be very similar.

One advantage of transposing moves is that you may arrive at a later point in the same opening variation you began with, but by playing a surprise move order you confuse your adversary. He may think you're trying to play something else. If so, it can unsettle his game, leading him astray.

CONCEPT: After starting with a particular opening, don't negate the possibility of favorable transformations to other systems by little turns and unexpected moves. It could have a powerful psychological effect on your opponent.

> **KASPAROV:** The strength of an innovation is that it forces the opponent to spend time on psychological regrouping, and any player knows how hard it is to switch from well-prepared analysis to specific spontaneous play.

In playing the English Opening **1. c4,** you are either trying to develop your game around controlling the square d5, or you are hoping to transpose to another opening in an unexpected way or at a more suitable moment.

Black retaliates with **1 . . . e6.**

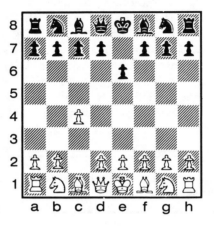

Q: Black's options: Which are still open? Which are closed?

Black would not likely flank his King-Bishop, for that entails moving the g-pawn, unnecessarily weakening f6. Once you've moved the e-pawn, the King-Bishop can be brought out without making another time-wasting pawn move. But Black still has other options. He can move his d-pawn two squares, or he can hold it back altogether. He can flank his Queen-Bishop at b7, to guard e4, creating the popular Queen's Indian Defense, or he can develop it through the center if he moves his d-pawn. He can even play the Dutch Defense, which involves the early movement of his King-Bishop pawn to f5, to control e4.

White continues **2. Nc3.**

Q: What plan does this reinforce?

White's Knight attacks e4 and overprotects d5, in conjunction with the c-pawn. If White wishes to pursue this plan further, he would flank his King-Bishop to g2 and play his Queen-pawn to d3.

Black essays **2 . . . d5.**

Q: Does Black have a threat?

It's certainly not to win a pawn by 3 . . . dxc4, for White regains the footman immediately with 4. Qa4 + (a fork) and 5. Qxc4. But Black can menacingly push his pawn to d4, dislodging White's Knight from its catbird seat. The response is a squelch.

White transposes to another opening with **3. d4.**

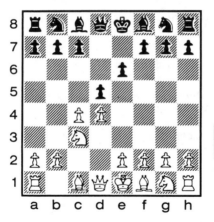

Q: What has this opening become, and what are some of its aims?

The opening is no longer an English—it's been transmogrified to a Queen's Gambit. Usually the same position is reached through a different order of moves: 1. d4 d5 2. c4 e6 3.Nc3. The distinctive thrust of the Queen's Gambit is White's second move, 2. c4. It is not a real gambit because White knows that if Black captures the c-pawn (2 . . . dxc4), Black cannot prevent White from winning it back. To keep a reasonable position, Black will have to abandon all attempts to hold the pawn, unless White plays feebly.

For example, after 1. d4 d5 2. c4 dxc4 3. e3 (not the best move but consistent for this instance) 3 . . . b5 (trying to protect the extra pawn) 4. a4 c6 5. axb5 cxb5 6. Qf3, Black's greediness costs him either a Knight or Bishop if he is to save his cornered Rook.

So White doesn't lose his c-pawn in the Queen's Gambit, but why does he play 2. c4? Surely to gain space on the Queenside and to pressure d5. Behind all this is the idea of compelling Black to take the c-pawn, removing his own d-pawn from the center. Once Black's d-pawn is seduced away, White will have two central pawns to Black's one. White then has the chance to mobilize that advantage, especially in the absence of Black's d-pawn, which is needed to ward off White's e-pawn. In the Queen's Gambit, White hopes to build solid central pressure through the advance of his c-pawn.

Black develops and defends with **3 . . . Nf6.**

Q: What is the relationship between center pawns and Knights in the opening?

Advancing the center pawns is important to Knights for two reasons:

A) They block certain squares, preventing their enemy counterparts from moving. This secures their own Knights, for the march of opposing pawns is anathema to Knights. The very expendable foot soldiers are really the only units able to drive opposing Knights away. Attacks from other chessmen will not usually compel a Knight to move if it is adequately protected. But however well protected a Knight is, the threat of capture by a single pawn is sufficient reason for it to flee.

B) They supply Knights with excellent support points, anchors in the opposing position from which to rest and ponder their next attacks.

White supports the center with **4. Nf3.**

Q: What other reasonable moves does White have here?

White could also bring out his Queen-Bishop, either to g5, where it pins a Knight, or to f4, where it reigns on the c7-g3 diagonal. Another possibility is the flanking 4. g3, designed to fianchetto the Bishop at g2, where, instead of occupying the center, the Bishop attacks it. White could try 4. e3, but this is unnecessarily passive and locks in his Queen-Bishop, it then being confined "inside the pawn chain."

CONCEPT: Try not to block your Bishops by placing pawns in their way. Develop your Bishops "outside their pawn chains."

Black builds with **4 . . . Be7.**

Q: This seems such a quiet move, how does it really help Black?

Quiet, yes, but it's also quite solid. At e7, the Bishop prevents the King-Knight from being pinned by White's dark-square Bishop. The move also prepares castling—if Black wishes to castle quickly, he can. Many players underrate the value of such steady, unassuming Bishop moves. They think that a move must accomplish something more forceful, such as engaging a piece immediately at the front, and that less spectacular plays should be deferred until necessary or they become more important in the scheme of things. But these "quiet" moves are actually essential to the preparation of a developing game.

CONCEPT: Don't shy away from "quiet" or modest moves. They are almost always necessary preludes to the fireworks that follow. They herald combination play.

White chooses **5. Bf4.**

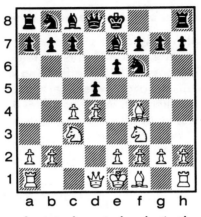

Q: In terms of central control, what's the difference between 5. Bg5 and 5. Bf4?

The development **5. Bf4** is concerned with dark-square control, whereas 5. Bg5 is directed at the light squares, because at g5 the Bishop assails a Knight that indeed guards light squares (e4 and d5). Since the Bishop would generally have the possibility of exchanging itself for the Knight—roughly an even trade—in doing so it would remove a useful protector of those light squares.

CONCEPT: A Bishop can influence squares of different color from those it controls by attacking enemy pieces that guard squares of other colors. One example is by exchanging itself for a Knight, which always guards different color squares from the one it occupies.

Black castles **5 . . . 0-0.**

Q: Is castling necessary?

No, but it's useful. By getting his King out of the center to safety behind a wall of pawns, Black prepares central operations that may lead to an opening of the game. With his King out of the way, his King-Rook can take advantage of the e-file, where it can snipe at the enemy King if the monarch remains in the middle.

White readies his King-Bishop with **6. e3.**

Q: *What does this move signify about White's light-square Bishop?*

That it won't be flanked, for 7. g3 weakens the light squares, is redundant, and deprives the dark-square Bishop of a haven at g3 or even h2, the diagonal then being blocked.

Black reacts with **6 . . . c5.**

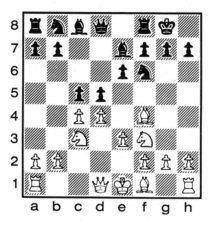

Q: *What is meant by this move?*

KOBLENTZ: Good lines of communication. These are the channels which permit our pieces to attack with maximum force and thus to penetrate into an opponent's territory.

Black, to take advantage of White's uncastled King, must open the game. Otherwise White will soon complete his development and secure the King on the Kingside. After **6 . . . c5,** the center radiates tension, and several exchanges are possible. The faster the exchanges, the sooner lines open for the pieces. This attack also provides Black's Queen with entry to the Queenside, at b6 or a5. Once Black moves his Queen off the d-file, he can shift his Rook there to harass White's Queen. Time is now critical.

CONCEPT: To open lines, exchange pawns. To keep the game closed, avoid exchanging pawns, especially in the center.

CONCEPT: If you are behind in development, keep the game closed. If you are ahead in development, open the game.

CONCEPT: If your King is stuck in the center, avoid exchanges that open the game for the enemy pieces to attack.

White takes a pawn **7. dxc5.**

Q: *Why does White capture this pawn?*

The capture avoids accepting an isolated d-pawn, generally a target for enemy pieces because no other pawn can guard it. White would receive such a weakness after a subsequent 7 . . . cxd4 8. exd4 dxc4. These exchanges would also lead to an opening of the e-file and potential threats to White's King.

Under the right circumstances, an isolated d-pawn can offer compensation, for it usually exists as the lone White pawn in the center versus a lone Black e-pawn. With the d-pawn at d4 and the e-pawn at e6, White tends to have greater space. Moreover, White's Knights, using the center pawn for support, may be able to assume posts deeper into Black's position than Black's Knights can occupy in White's. A pawn at d4 supports pieces at e5 and c5, while a pawn at e6 supports pieces at d5 and f5. Nevertheless, the isolated d-pawn could conceivably come under heavy fire from Black's pieces along the open d-file and elsewhere. Such a pawn is a double-edged sword. It has good or bad points, depending on the merits of a given position.

CONCEPT: Accept isolated d-pawns if the attacking possibilities they provide outweigh their inherent weakness. Avoid them if they provide too little compensation to offset their vulnerability.

Black takes back the pawn **7 . . . Bxc5.**

Q: *Should White exchange pawns, 8. cxd5 exd5, saddling Black with an isolated d-pawn?*

It would be inadvisable. Black's resulting isolated d-pawn would not really be weak. The exchange actually improves Black's game and attacking chances:

A) It opens the e-file for the King-Rook.
B) It clears the c8-h3 diagonal for the Queen-Bishop.
C) It affords Black the possibility of a further advance to d4, after suitable preparation, possibly opening the game further.

White plays **8. Qc2.**

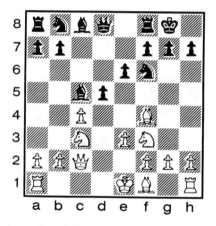

Q: *What does this do?*

A) It develops a piece, though in the opening not the most desirable one.
B) It avoids moving the King-Bishop for a second time, as in the line 8. Be2 dxc4 9. Bxc4, though the tempo loss is not critical.
C) It clears the d-file for a Rook, though White may not have time to capitalize on this for a while.
D) It makes castling Queenside possible, though that could be risky.
E) It seizes the b1-h7 diagonal.
F) It guards c3 in case of future pins.
G) It veils a potential discovery to the Bishop at c5.

Black builds with **8 . . . Nc6.**

Q: What move must White guard against?

White must be vigilant against a timely attack from Black at b4. This sortie, executed at the right moment, might prove quite disconcerting, for White would have to expend a tempo to salvage his Queen.

White stands sentinel with **9. a3.**

Q: Is there a threat here?

White may be able to launch a Queenside offensive with 10. b4, when White's cadre of three pawns will guard important squares and expropriate vast terrain.

Black replies **9 . . . Qa5.**

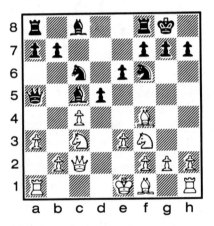

Q: Doesn't this leave Black open to a pawn fork at b4?

At an apropos moment, yes, but not here. If 10. b4?, either 10 . . . Nxb4 or 10 . . . Bxb4 wins a pawn, for White's a-pawn is pinned and unable to capture on b4 without exposing its Rook to Black's Queen. Black's move does a few things: It clears the d-file for a Black Rook, and it pins White's Knight at c3 to its king.

CONCEPT: Develop your pieces so that they exercise multiple functions. This confers more options and greater flexibility.

White peers at the center with **10. Rd1.**

Q: How does this imperil Black?

White suddenly plans 11. b4, forking Black's Queen and Bishop. With the a-pawn no longer pinned, White's free to capture on b4. The centralization of the Rook also intensifies the pressure against d5, and if Black lets down his guard, White may be able to filch a pawn.

Black solidifies with **10 . . . Be7.**

Q: How does this shore up Black's game?

It avoids the planned fork at b4, and it removes the Bishop from the c-file, where lurk future discoveries. It also strengthens f6 and d8.

White inches up with **11. Rd2.**

Q. What does he have in mind?

White apparently wishes to unpin his Knight, which after **11. Rd2** is free to move. Unfortunately, it's an unsatisfactory approach to the problem. Instead of **11. Rd2** White should have tried 11. Nd2. This breaks the pin while guarding against Knight invasions at e4. And from d2, White's Knight can transfer to b3, shooing away Black's Queen, totally dismantling the pin. This defensive maneuver is typical when the Black Queen induces early pins in Queen-pawn openings. It has some drawbacks in removing a Knight from a more central post and spending a couple of tempi. Yet White should do something about the pin before it becomes a serious problem.

KASPAROV: The excessive reinforcement of one point inevitably leads to a weakness of control over others.

CONCEPT: If you have acceptable options, don't un-necessarily place your pieces in pins. It could pall your entire game and backfire, reducing your efforts to mere defense.

CONCEPT: If one of your pieces is pinned, try to break the pin as soon as reasonably possible. Otherwise, you may not be able to utilize the pinned piece when you need it. Furthermore, you may lose the services of other pieces that are tapped for defense.

Black forges ahead with **11 . . . Ne4.**

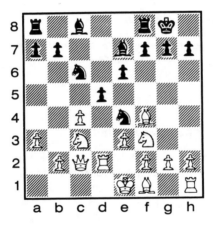

Q: Doesn't this lose a pawn?

The pawn is a sacrifice, not a loss. Black hopes that the time lost in capturing the offered pawn can be used to propel his attack. A leitmotif of Black's aggression is the pin on White's Rook, which will cost the defender even more time. White could have averted muddy waters by playing 11. Nd2 instead of **11. Rd2.**

White takes Black's Knight **12. Nxe4.**

> **POLUGAEVSKY:** Be prepared to give up material for active play.

Q: Could White avoid this capture and play 12. Rd3?

This fails utterly to 12 . . . dxc4, winning a pawn and gaining valuable time by attacking the Rook, which, situated at d3, obstructs the light-square Bishop's defense of c4.

Black retakes the Knight **12 . . . dxe4.**

Q: Should White reject the gambit and play 13. Nd4?

After 13. Nd4 e5 14. Nxc6 bxc6 15. Bg3 f5, Black's pawns are ominous. If White can't see concrete reasons for ignoring the gambit—if he thinks he can get away with it—he should take the pawn. Since he is behind in development and King safety, it's risky, but it's the only conceivable way for him to achieve a compensating advantage.

CONCEPT: In many positions, to get an advantage—maybe just to stay with it—you might have to take a chance in order to gain superiority. Otherwise, you could be saddled with a passive, lifeless game.

> **KARPOV:** It's dangerous to maintain equality at the cost of placing the pieces passively.

CONCEPT: In a fairly balanced position, you don't gain one kind of advantage without ceding another kind of approximate equal value. Such transactions must be quid pro quo.

White, to compensate for his inferior position, must accept the pawn sacrifice, consolidate by castling and completing his development, and trade down, heading for the endgame, where the extra pawn should be significant. This early in the game it's less important to have an extra pawn than later on, with fewer pieces on the board.

White accepts the gambit by **13. Qxe4.**

Q: Is White now able to break the pin with 14. b4?

This ends the pin, but hangs the a-pawn to Black's Queen, after which Black's minor pieces (Bishop and Knight) count on a field day on the Queenside.

Black takes the d-file with **13 . . . Rd8.**

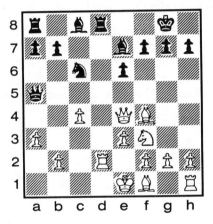

Q: How would you evaluate the move 14. c5?

It's an interesting resource, flawed in that White surrenders the extra pawn. Black's capture, however, means he will relinquish the pin, allowing White to coordinate his forces and shuttle his King to safety. For example, after 14. c5 Qxc5 15. Bd3 (threatening mate in two moves) 15 . . . f5 16. Qc4, White may even be a little better. If Black avoids the Queen trade, White will castle. Of course, it would be an error to play 14 . . . Bxc5 instead of 14 . . . Qxc5, for White then forks Bishop and Queen with 15. b4. By giving back the gambit pawn, White can break the force of Black's attack.

CONCEPT: If you are under attack but ahead in material, you might choose to give back some or all of the material if it disrupts your opponent's assault and leads to equality or some nonmaterial type of superiority.

CONCEPT: To maintain an overall advantage, it may not be necessary to retain specific types of advantage. You may be able to stay on top by converting one advantage into another. If you have a material edge, you might be able to trade that for an advantage in space and time, thereby having an overall superiority based on having the initiative, for example.

White retreats his Queen **14. Qc2.**

Q: Is this White's best move?

Hardly. White should return the pawn by 14. c5!. The other move wastes time. It doesn't even develop a new piece, so that White is no closer to castling.

Black advances **14 . . . e5.**

Q: What does this thrust do?

It gains time by attacking the Bishop, and clears the c8-h3 diagonal for Black's light-square Bishop.

CONCEPT: You gain time in chess by completing an action in fewer moves than it should normally take, or by making your opponent respond to your moves. If you can improve your position as he wastes time responding, you've gained time.

White saves his Bishop by **15. Bg3.**

Q: What is Black's plan?

Black has the initiative—the ability to attack—and looks to convert that into something greater, like a mating net or winning material. He therefore will try to retard White's development by forcing White to respond with other than development by forcing White to respond with other than developing moves. A key in the attack is the pin on White's Rook, which further hampers normal development, for White must certify that his Rook is adequately protected. His pieces are tied to the Rook's defense.

CONCEPT: If you have the initiative, try to increase it by gaining in development while deterring your opponent from completing his own. Usually, threat after threat should be generated to keep your opponent off balance with no chance to consolidate his game.

MAKOGONOV: The momentum of the attack must not be allowed to slacken.

Black sustains his attack with **15 . . . e4.**

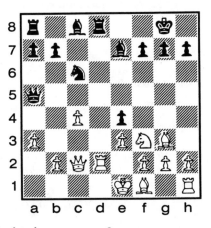

Q: Doesn't this lose a pawn?

Black does not lose a pawn, but sacrifices one. White will have to take it with his Queen. This will waste even more time, for it's generally unproductive to move the same piece over and over. If he didn't have to respond to these consistent threats, White would build his game and castle.

CONCEPT: Try not to move the same piece too often, especially in the opening, where all the forces should be mobilized. In particular, avoid overusing the Queen. It needs assistance from other pieces, and the faster they're brought out the better.

White takes the interloper **16. Qxe4.**

ALEKHINE: It is quite evident that such displacements of the Queen at an early stage in the opening are not likely to reap any advantage.

Q: How should Black continue his blitz?

By developing with a gain of time. He can bring out his Queen Bishop, attacking White's Queen and forcing it to move once again. Thus, another move goes by and White is still unable to get out his light-square Bishop, break the pin to his Rook, or come any closer to castling.

Black proceeds with **16 . . . Bf5.**

Q: How would you evaluate this position?

White is up two pawns, but on Black's side of the ledger is a lead in development, open lines for his pieces, the initiative, a safer King's position, and an irritating pin on the enemy Rook. The overall advantage rests with Black.

White saves his Queen by **17. Qf4.**

Q: Why does White move the Queen to f4?

Look closely. It's the only safe square the Queen has. Moving to any other square exposes it to capture.

Black exchanges Rook **17 . . . Rxd2.**

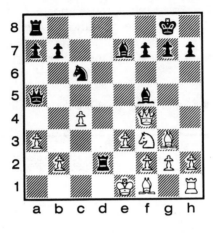

Q: Since Black is attacking, why does he trade pieces? Won't that dissipate his onslaught?

Generally, it would. But here Black wants to exploit the pin along the a5-e1 diagonal. This he does by exchanging pieces and hauling up fresh troops that White can't quite match. Black's second Rook stands poised to enter the fray. White's is stranded in the corner. So the trade actually enables Black to capitalize on his superior development.

TAL: Speed of development is the first priority, and the open position renders each extra tempo especially valuable.

White recoups his Rook **18. Nxd2.**

Q: What is Black's natural continuation?

Black should develop his last piece, the Queen-Rook to d8. Even though White can defend against the threatened mate, the force of Black's attack is swelling.

Black continues **18 . . . Rd8.**

> **KOBLENTZ:** The attack has to be aimed at a target or weakness in the enemy King position.

Q: *How can White save his Knight?*

Here the real problem of the pin is highlighted. The Knight is stuck, unable to move to safety; it must be defended. White can play 19. b4, but after 19 . . . Qxa3, his game falls apart, for the b-pawn then hangs, while 20. Qxf5 encounters 20 . . . Qc1 +.

White empowers the Queen to defend the Knight with **19. e4.**

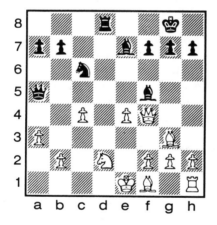

Black rejoins **19 . . . Bg4!**

> **KOBLENTZ:** The hallmark of attacking games consists not only in that the defender constantly has to solve difficult problems, but also that the attacker must always concentrate hard on the search for new attacking possibilities.

Q: Can't White simply take the Bishop with his Queen?

Bad move. Taking the Bishop terminates the Queen's protection of the Knight at d2. Meanwhile Black has some dangerous possibilities. On one hand he threatens 20 . . . Bg5, skewering White's Queen and Knight; the Bishop is immune, protected by the Queen at a5. Black also envisions 20 . . . Bb4, when 21. axb4. Qa1+ 22 Nb1 Rd1 is mate. Black's position is so strong, it bristles with surging attack.

CONCEPT: If you know you have a powerful game, but don't see a definite resolution to the attack, examine the position carefully. In such situations, the "laws of chess" insure that tactics and combinations must be there, no matter how latent or concealed. You're justified in looking for them.

White clings to hope with **20. c5.**

Q: How does this help White?

It prevents 20 . . . Bg5, for the Queen's defense of that square is cut by the pawn on c5. It also delays, for at least a move, . . . Bb4. White also, perhaps, gets the opportunity for 21. Bc4, preparing castling, attacking f7, and readying the Bishop to intercede at d5, in order to shut out Black's Rook.

Black offers a piece with **20 . . . Nb4!.**

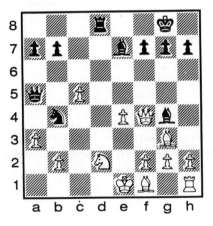

> **KOBLENTZ: No price is too great for the scalp of the enemy King.**

Q: Are both Black's Knight and Bishop at g4 invulnerable to capture?

Yes indeed:

A) If 21. axb4, then 21 . . . Qa1+ 22. Nb1 Rd1 is mate.
B) And if 21. Qxg4, then 21 . . . Nc2+ 22. Ke2 Qxd2+ 23. Kf3 Ne1 is also mate.
C) Moreover, Black perceives mate by 21 . . . Nc2.

White shields d1 by **21. f3.**

Q: Does 21 . . . Nc2+ make sense?

On 21 . . . Nc2+, White must move his King, but he still has some fight in him after 22. Kd1, planning to usurp the Knight. Though White's position would still be quite precarious, Black needs to—and can—discombobulate the White forces even further.

CONCEPT: If you have strong attacking possibilities that don't seem to lead to anything concrete, you may want to hold them in reserve and build your game even more. A move or two later, conditions on the board may be different and may suddenly explode into palpable advantage—the win of material or a mating attack.

> **BOTVINNIK: Everything is in a state of flux, and this includes the world of chess.**

Black blindsides White with **21 . . . g5!**

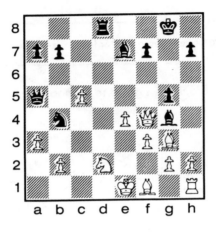

Q: *How does this move trap the Queen?*

The Queen has no safe place to move that also copes with the deadly threats against d2. For example:

A) If 22. Qe3, then 22 . . . Nc2+ forks the Queen and King.
B) If 22. Qc7 or 22. Qe5, then 22 . . . Nc2+ and White is mated in a few moves, either of several ways.
C) And if 22. Qxg4, again 22 . . . Nc2+ is decisive.

White submits with **22. axb4.**

Q: *Doesn't this just lose the Queen to 22 . . . gxf4?*

Yes, but not on the 22nd move, for Black's own Queen is menaced. After 22. axb4 Black must first check on the back rank and then he can take the opposing Queen. At this point, White should actually resign.

Black frolics along with **22 . . . Qa1+.**

Q: *Should White sidle his King to e2 or f2?*

In either case White's is a lost cause. Moving to e2 blocks in the King-Bishop, and therefore the Rook, but adds protection to the Knight at d2, which will soon face further attack. White must make the best of a losing situation.

White plays **23. Ke2.**

Q: By how much will Black be ahead after taking White's Queen?

After 23 . . . gxf4 24. Bxf4, for example, Black's extra Queen is not quite offset by White's three plus pawns and additional Knight. In practical terms, White would be down by at least a minor piece, and that's putting it mildly.

Black takes the Queen **23 . . . . gxf4.**

Q: Is it better to play 24. Bxf4 or 24. fxg4?

SPASSKY: In this situation one move is as good as another.

Neither one is particularly more resistant. After 24. fxg4 fxg3 25. hxg3 Qxb2, White's future is no less bleak. At least by keeping his dark-square Bishop on board he might be able to uphold d2.

White struggles on with **24. Bxf4.**

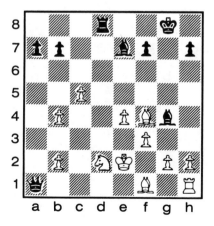

Q: How should Black now proceed?

When you have such an overwhelming advantage, there's really no need to take any chances. You should simply consolidate, knowing full well that you will win easily if it comes to an endgame. You should, however, play to maximize your attack without risk, because it may still be possible to catch the enemy King quickly.

Black saves his Bishop by **24 . . . Be6.**

Q: What else does this repositioning do?

It places the Bishop on a diagonal which may lead to a check at c4, when desirable. It also removes two squares from the enemy Knight. Thus it consolidates as it propels Black's attack.

White transfers his Bishop **25. Be5.**

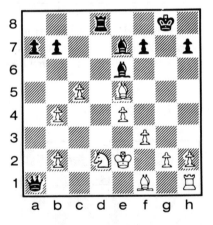

Q: Is there another point to this move?

To defend the b-pawn against Black's Queen. In order to guard both d2 and b2, the Bishop can set up at c3. But this is to no avail as well.

Black moves in with **25 . . . Qc1.**

Q: What can be said about White's light-square Bishop and Rook?

Because they have no way to participate in the game, they might as well be absent. In effect, on top of all his other woes, White is behind by an extra Rook and Bishop. Note how White's Knight, thanks to **24 . . . Be6,** lacks a safe move.

White defends with **26. Bc3.**

Q: How can Black bring more pressure to bear on d2?

Black's dark-square Bishop can shift to g5, where it attacks the Knight, guards e3, and hooks up with the Queen along the c1-h6 diagonal.

Black indeed plays **26 . . . Bg5.**

White Resigns.

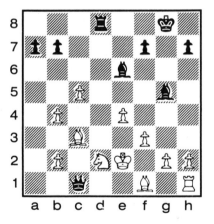

POSTSCRIPT

White gradually got into trouble, first by unnecessarily putting his Rook in a pin, and then by wasting precious time in taking a gambit pawn and failing to return it at the right moment. Black utilized the pawn sacrifice to open lines and to increase his initiative, step by step. After a point, White's King was under constant threat, never able to castle. White's situation grew worse in that he couldn't find the time to bring out his King-Bishop and Rook. Black wisely used all his pieces, rather than playing with a fragmented army as White did.

The phases of the attack are interesting. Black's initial sacrifices were light, involving only pawns, and they were made to give Black the initiative. As the attack developed, the bribes became greater, with various pieces being offered up for sacrifice. An overriding theme was the decoying away of White's Queen. Eventually, it got so entangled in a defensive web, it became trapped and was lost. In the end, Black's superior mobility (thanks to control of the lines he had opened and utilized), enabled him to attack with ease on both flanks and provoke White's downfall.

Weak Pawns, Position Play, and the Endgame

WHITE: Vaganjan
BLACK: Nogueiras
Montpelier Candidates 1985

WHAT TO LOOK FOR

In this game we see the consistent execution of a plan, involving careful selection, appropriate preparation, and incisive implementation. White early on saddles Black with weak pawns, accentuates their vulnerability, squelches counterplay, and engineers a winning endgame. Along the way, several important ideas are illustrated.

PAWN ISLANDS

A *pawn island* is a group of pawns belonging to one player that are separated from other friendly pawns by an empty file. Generally, the more pawn islands, the harder it is to defend them. The fewer islands, the better. Black here incurs these weaknesses and pays for it.

ROOK-AND-PAWN ENDGAME PRINCIPLES

In order to win this game, White must capitalize on his superiority in the endgame. He relies most on centralization of the King, activation of his Rook, hampering of the enemy Rook, infliction of additional weaknesses and targets, and the use of *zugzwang*, which refers to situations where you are compelled to move, worsening your position. In a *zugzwang* position, you'd rather not move, but you have no choice.

> SMYSLOV: Nowhere does logic of thought reveal itself so clearly as in the concluding stage of the game.

THE TACTICS OF POSITION PLAY

Don't scour the moves for fireworks here. You won't discover any combinative bombshells. Instead we uncover a wealth of subtle maneuvering, the use of finesse, and hidden and sophisticated nuances of position play. In other words, playing for small advantages. This all ties back to the correct choice of plan, a hallmark of the developing Soviet school.

White begins **1. d4.**

Q: Why does a Queen-pawn opening tend to produce a slower, more positional game than a King-pawn opening?

Mainly because a Queen-pawn game is less likely to open up. With a King-pawn opener it's easier to advance both center pawns two squares each. This way you can more likely exchange some pawns, clearing paths through the center—hence an open game. If you can't exchange so easily or at all, the game remains more blocked and develops more slowly.

If you begin by moving your e-pawn, you can practically count on being able to follow at some later point with d4, for the d-pawn starts the game with the great natural protector, the Queen. After 1. e4 e5, White can play 2. d4, with hopes of an open game. And, if Black captures White's pawn 2 . . . exd4,

White can choose to take back at once by 3. Qxd4. White can open the game without having to sacrifice a pawn.

But if you begin by moving the d-pawn first **1. d4,** Black can actually make it undesirable to move your other center pawn two squares on the next move by 1 . . . d5, for the e-pawn advances without any backing. This doesn't mean that Queen-pawn openings can't produce open games (games with free and easy movement through the center). But it may very well be harder to open up such games.

CONCEPT: If you enjoy slower, more maneuvering games, play d-pawn openings. They generally take longer to open up.

Black answers **1 . . . Nf6.**

Q: Does Black have to challenge the square e4?

This is only one way to stop White from continuing 2. e4, creating a classical pawn center. Other ways to thwart it directly are 1 . . . d5 and 1 . . . f5. All three first moves attack the square e4. An entirely different approach is to allow White to establish a center, say by 1 . . . g6 2. e4, and then try to pressure it indirectly, eventually forcing White to weaken the center by ill-considered advances, or to abandon it completely through exchanges. This modern approach is extremely popu-lar with the young Russians.

POLUGAEVSKY: In chess, as in other types of sport, there are constant discussions about the young, about the changing of the old guard, and about the different generations. The young are condescendingly slapped on the back, then scolded, and then raised up almost to the heavens. In all of this the basic argument used is competitive results: the places occupied and the points scored. But you know, in chess there is always a highly objective criterion—the moves of the game. And it is more accurate to compare not the number of wins of players past and present, but the quality of those wins, and not the degree of knowledge, but the degree of individual creativity.

CONCEPT: If in the opening you allow your opponent to build a pawn center, take steps to undermine it with pressure from the flanks and from off center. Forcing the pawns to advance prematurely may weaken them and subject them to attack.

CONCEPT: If your opponent permits you to create a pawn center in the opening, develop your pieces around it and make sure it's secure. Don't push your pawns too quickly, and if you do advance them, enlist support for them beforehand.

White continues **2. Nf3.**

Q: Does this move give White options that 2. c4 doesn't?

This is a solid but more passive continuation than 2. c4. White may be content to complete his Kingside development and castle. One system White could still play is the Colle (1. d4 d5 2. Nf3 Nf6 3. e3), which could be arrived at by transposition after 3. e3. The scheme is to play 4. Bd3 and later advance the e-pawn. If White's d-pawn is attacked by a subsequent 4 . . .c5, he can play 5. c3. White retains this option of strengthening his center by such c-pawn protection. With preparation, he can later advance his e-pawn. Once he's played 2. c4, however, the Colle is no longer possible.

CONCEPT: Pawn moves are irreversible. Even if you have the time, you can't take them back. Be chary of making them, however innocent they seem.

Black opens the f8-a3 diagonal with **2 . . . e6.**

Q: What does Black's move hint about his Queen-Bishop?

Since it blocks the c8-h3 diagonal even further—cutting down on the light-square Bishop's scope—it implies that the Bishop might secure a more promising post by developing toward the flank. Thus, after a subsequent 3 . . . b6, Black could slide the Bishop to b7 or a6.

White rejoins **3. c4.**

Q: *Wouldn't it be better to play for an immediate e4 by 3. Nc3?*

It's a reasonable idea, but 3. Nc3 is surely not better than 3. c4. Now is it certain that White can enforce a subsequent e4. Black could rebuff the immediate thrust by 3 . . . d5. An even more telling drawback is that the c-pawn becomes blocked, making it harder for White to find room for his pieces on the Queenside. It's also more likely the game will remain closed. Still, it's not a terrible move.

Black flanks with **3 . . . b6.**

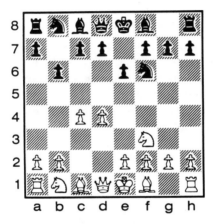

Q: *What opening does this move characterize?*

Regardless whether Black develops his light-square Bishop to b7 or a6, his third move distinguishes the Queen's Indian Defense. For years it was thought to be a modest, unassuming approach to the center, where Black defers central occupation until completing his development. White, too, played it positionally, hoping for a slight but long-term edge. The opening in recent years, however, has undergone an overhaul—thanks to the new world champion, Gary Kasparov, who has sharpened it into a deadly attacking weapon.

CONCEPT: Don't be afraid to study and play older openings which have simply gone out of style. By meshing the best of the old with the best of the new, you may come away with a sound opening repertoire that few study and therefore few can analyze.

ESTRIN: The young player should not concentrate his attention on the most popular openings, which are constantly practiced by the leading players, but should gradually master and include in his repertoire other openings which suit his individual style.

White fianchettos his King-Bishop **4. g3.**

Q: Are there other reasonable tries for White?

Among the moves played with success here are 4. e3, with the idea of developing the light-square Bishop to d3; 4. Bg5, temporarily influencing the squares d5 and e4 by pinning the Black Knight that guards them; and 4. a3, the Petrosian System, which stops the future pin on White's Knight after it moves to c3. The latter approach is the cherished system of Gary Kasparov.

Black sidles with **4 . . . Ba6.**

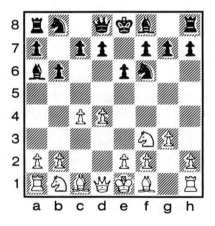

Q. What's the point of this move, and how does it differ from 4 . . . Bb7?

After 4 . . . Bb7, Black plans to guard d5 and e4, while neutralizing White's own fianchettoed Bishop. Very often the two Bishops are eventually exchanged. With 4 . . . Ba6, Black wants to capitalize on the removal of White's Bishop from the a6-f1 diagonal. Instead of the Bishop defending the assailed c-pawn, White will have to conjure another watchdog for it.

White enlivens the game with **5. Qb3.**

Q: What asset, if any, does this move have over 5. b3?

The move 5. b3 has its points, but it slightly weakens the Queenside dark-squares a3 and c3. Moreover, it blocks the White Queen's avenue to the Queenside. On the other hand, at b3, the Queen is susceptible to attack (Nb8-c6-a5, for example). Even good moves have dark facets.

Black, as expected, plays **5 . . . Nc6.**

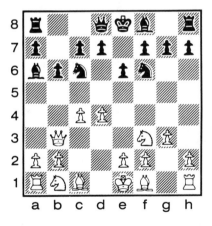

Q: What is Black's threat?

Black wants to play 6 . . . Na5, forking the Queen and c-pawn, winning the hapless foot soldier.

CONCEPT: Knights are usually not well placed on the edge of the board, except occasionally when they are in closed positions where the center is blocked. In other situations you may want to temporarily move them to the flank to gain some advantage before transferring them back to the center (such as the contingency of Na5-c4, to the flank and back). This contradicts the popular notion that "a Knight on the rim is dim." Sometimes it's as luminous on the flank as anywhere else.

KASPAROV: It is not rules that have to be reckoned with, but exceptions to them.

White fortifies his c-pawn by **6. Nb-d2.**

Q: Can't Black still play 6 . . . Na5, swiping at White's Queen?

Yes, it's reasonable. After 6 . . . Na5 7. Qc2, Black might follow with 7 . . . c5, increasing tension in the center and preventing 8. b4, dislodging the Knight from its perch.

CONCEPT: To safeguard a Knight from enemy pawn attack, guard the attack squares with your own pawns. For example, you can stabilize a Black Knight at c5 from a White pawn's attack at b4 by playing a Black pawn to a5.

Black pins White's Knight by **6 . . . Bb4.**

Q: Should White now play 7. Bg2?

Not unless he desires a little trouble. After 7. Bg2, Black has 7 . . . Ne4!, and Black has latent threats against d2 and d4 that compel White to play with super caution. It's easy to peck away at pinned pieces.

White advances **7. d5.**

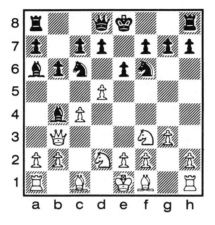

Q: What's inevitable after this move?

Black is forced to exchange his dark-square Bishop for White's Knight. Otherwise the Bishop is lost to White's Queen after Black moves his c6-Knight. Note how at b3, White's Queen is able to guard d5, whereas at d1 the Queen's protection for d5 would be lopped off by the Knight at d2.

Black takes the Knight **7 . . . Bxd2 + .**

Q: Should Black have interposed 7 . . . exd5 before clobbering the Knight?

By trading pawns first, Black confers on White a two-to-one pawn majority in the center. White also derives an open c-file. By not taking the d-pawn, Black keeps White's c-pawn sitting there as a potential target.

White retakes **8. Bxd2.**

Q: If Black now plays 8 . . . Na5, how does the position stand after 9. Bxa5 bxa5?

Pluses for White are the superior space, possible play against the doubled a-pawns, and some attacking chances along the open lines. Minuses are that Black attains an open b-file for his Rooks, some pressure against White's overextended pawns, and the contingency of using his doubled a-pawn as a battering ram against White's Queenside pawns if they move, creating further weaknesses.

Black brazens **8 . . . Na5.**

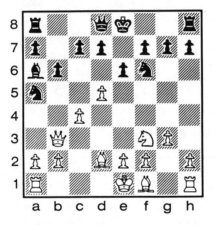

Q: What two things is Black threatening?

KARPOV: The fact that a Knight is temporarily on the edge of the board is of no great significance.

The obvious threat is the capture of White's Queen or c-pawn. But Black is also eyeing White's d-pawn, which is attacked twice.

White unveils **9. Qa4!.**

> **ALEKHINE:** A most effective square for the Queen, from which this piece will exert a troublesome pressure upon Black's Queen's wing.

Q: Is White's c-pawn immune?

Black is unable to capture it safely. If 9 . . . Bxc4, then 10. Bxa5 bxa5 11. Qxc4 wins the Bishop. And if 9 . . . Nxc4, then 10. Qxa6 again wins the Bishop.

Black centralizes with **9 . . . Ne4.**

Q: What's the threat?

In addition to 10 . . . Nxd2, Black scents the possibility of 9 . . . Nc5, chasing the Queen and winning the c-pawn.

White expropriates the Knight **10. Bxa5.**

Q: Should White have interposed 10. dxe6 before capturing the Knight?

Why? Black would take the pawn back 10 . . . fxe6, getting an open f-file and a central pawn majority. White shouldn't readily trade his powerful d-pawn, which stifles Black considerably.

> **PETROSIAN:** Up to a particular moment I would follow a definite line, and then doubts would come up and I would move off the right track. This is what happened on this occasion [Donner 1966]. After a well-thought-out plan, I contemplated something different, but then changed my mind and returned to the original idea. Luckily, my advantage this time was so great that nothing unexpected happened.

CONCEPT: Don't exchange if it eases pressure on your opponent's game. Keep him cramped.

CONCEPT: Don't break a sequence of moves with another set of moves unless it's clearly necessary or contributes to the initial variation. Introducing secondary moves may eventually stymie the satisfactory completion of the first sequence.

Black takes back **10 . . . bxa5.**

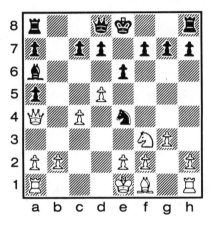

ALEKHINE: Black is not concerned about the possibility of doubled pawns. The open b-file would constitute compensation for the slight weakness.

Q: Why not 11. Qxa5?

Taking Black's a-pawn abandons the c-pawn to 11 . . . Bxc4. It's a no-no to exchange a healthy pawn for a sickly one, which will probably be won anyway later on. And even if White can't overtake it, Black's forces would be taxed in its defense.

CONCEPT: Avoid exchanging your strengths for your opponent's weaknesses. Instead, consider his liabilities as targets to be won later or to serve as defensive albatrosses.

White interposes **11. dxe6!.**

Q: How does this exchange increase White's tactical possibilities?

It clears the h1-a8 diagonal of pawns so that White's Kingside Bishop can ambush Black's Queen-Rook. Otherwise, Black might exchange on d5 himself, keeping the diagonal blocked with a White pawn.

Black evens the score with **11 . . . fxe6.**

Q: Does Black get any counter-advantages after this exchange?

Surely. For one he gets an open f-file for his Rook after castling. Secondly, he now has a majority of two central pawns to one, which portend possibly greater opportunities in the center proper. There are two sides to every coin.

White continues **12. Bg2.**

Q: Is there a threat here?

White plans to uncover an attack against the Knight at e4 by moving his own Knight at f3. Black's problem could be compounded because of the potential pin along the g2-a8 diagonal.

Black castles **12 . . . 0-0.**

Q: What does this do to White's immediate plan?

It frustrates it, for if White moves his Knight now, he exposes his f-pawn to capture by Black's Knight and Rook. Black's counterplay may be more than White bargains for. Temporarily, Black seems safe.

White also castles **13. 0-0.**

Q: Who has the edge and why?

Material is even, and both Kings appear safe. The forces are about equally developed, but Black's function slightly less harmoniously. There seems to be no cooperation, for example, between Black's Bishop and Knight. Such units, when scattered and not supported, are subject to combinations, especially when the attacker sports a sprightly Queen. Black gives some pressure along the f-file, while White threatens on the long diagonal leading to a8. A key difference is pawn structure. White's is more organic, arranged in only two blocks, from a2-c4, and from e2-h2. Black's pawns are divided into three groups: from h7-g7, from e6-c7, and the two isolated a-pawns, both weak and vulnerable. White's slight lead is better.

CONCEPT: In developing your pieces, get them working together harmoniously. Don't place them at cross purposes, alone with no support. That's how you can lose them.

Black plays **13 . . . Rb8.**

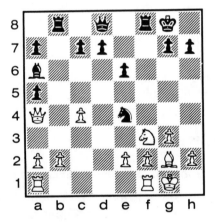

Q: Couldn't Black instead defend his a-pawn by moving the c-pawn?

Sometimes the cure is worse than the disease. By playing 13 . . . c6 (more dangerous is 13 . . . c5 because the pin along the g2-a8 diagonal here is serious), Black weakens his control of important squares on the d-file, especially d6, which then will lack pawn support for the entire game. White can intensify his pressure along the d-file by occupying it with one or two Rooks. This, in conjunction with a Knight attack from e5, brings no relief. The move 13 . . . Rb8 at least gets the Rook off the questioned diagonal with a time-gaining threat, because White will have to save his menaced b-pawn. For now, the a-pawn is immune in that White's own c-pawn is still under attack.

White jumps ahead with **14. Ne5!**.

Q: What are White's two most significant threats?

In this double attack, White threatens the Knight at e4 with his Bishop and the pawn at d7 with his Queen and Knight. If he could play 15. Nxd7, his Knight would be forking Black's two Rooks. That would win the exchange, a Knight for a Rook.

Black goes on his own Rook hunt with **14 . . . Nd2**.

Q: Doesn't 15. Rf-d1 now win material?

It may look that way, in that Black's Knight at d2 and pawn at d7 are both attacked. But Black has the resource 15 . . . Rxb2, which protects the Knight and avoids the fork of Rooks. The position is still extremely complicated, and White may have the advantage, but why try something less than certain when you have a choice?

CONCEPT: If you have an edge, clarify; if you are behind, complicate.

White snatches Black's d-pawn **15. Nxd7**.

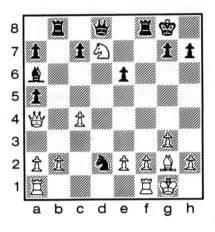

Q: Should Black pin White's Knight by 15 . . . Qe8?

Only if he wants to lose the game. After 15 . . . Qe8 16. Bc6 (among other sixteenth moves for White), White gains time to win material because of the sudden threat to Black's Queen by 17. Nf6 +, unleashing a discovery to it from the Bishop.

Black follows with **15 . . . Nxf1.**

Q: Of the two Rooks, which one should White's Knight capture?

Though captures have their merits and demerits, the determining factor is that by capturing the King-Rook, White will divert Black's Queen from the Queenside weaknesses, exposing them to dangers. To avoid capturing on f8 with his Queen, Black's King would have to take back on f8 instead. So placed, it suddenly becomes more vulnerable.

White expropriates the King-Rook **16. Nxf8.**

Q: What do you think of the desperado (a tactic in which a piece about to be captured "sells its life dearly" by first exchanging it for something of lesser value) **16 . . . Nxh2?**

The tactic fails to 17. Nxe6, when 17 . . . Qe7 18. Kxh2 Qxe6 drops the Queen to 19. Bd5. A desperado is a tactic known as an "in-between move." Since they could easily backfire, one must calculate desperados carefully. An unexpected resource can change everything.

Black beheads the Knight **16 . . . Qxf8.**

Q: How should White recapture on f1?

Taking back with the King is potentially dangerous. Taking with the Bishop removes that weapon from its glorious diagonal. That leaves the Rook (which needs to be developed) to fill the place of its captured partner at f1.

White tidies up with **17. Rxf1.**

Q: Can't Black now regain the pawn by 17 . . . Rxb2?

Yes, but the consequences are 18. Qc6!, when White starts to take advantage of the disorganized Black Queenside. More than that, White's Queen would exert an enormous restraining influence over the whole of Black's game.

Black offers a trade with **17 . . . Qb4.**

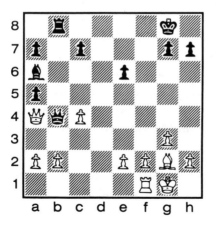

> **ALEKHINE:** Black concludes that his position will be more easily defendable after the exchange of Queens.

Q: Is the Queen trade essentially forced?

Does White have another choice? If he protects his Queen, Black captures it and then wins back at least a pawn. If White hustles the Queen away, Black's pieces capture either on b2 or c4, depending on which transaction is more appropriate.

White swaps Queens **18. Qxb4.**

Q: Should Black now take back with his a-pawn, straightening out his pawn formation?

It certainly should be considered. But after 18 . . . axb4 19. b3 Rd8 20. a3! bxa3 21. Ra1, White gains access to Black's isolated pawns. As Bobby Fischer once remarked, such pawns tend to fall like "ripe apples."

So Black captures with his Rook, **18 . . . Rxb4.**

Q: How can White defend both his c-pawn and his b-pawn?

By playing **19. b3,** which he does.

Q: Can Black try to undermine this structure?

Black can advance his doubled a-pawn to a4 and exchange it for White's b-pawn. If White then defends his b-pawn with his Rook from b1, Black wins a pawn by Bxc4, exploiting the pin along the b-file.

CONCEPT: If you have doubled pawns, try to exchange them for healthy ones. If you are attacking your opponent's doubled pawns, try to prevent him from exchanging them off for pawns of your own. You don't want to exchange pawns; you want to win pawns.

Black continues **19 . . . a4.**

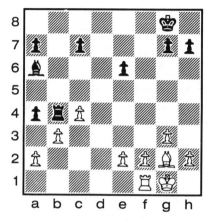

Q: In light of the previous discussion, should White play 20. bxa4, or surrender his b-pawn and instead seize the d-file?

The blunder 20. bxa4 leads to a totally shattered pawn structure, while seizure of the d-file with his Rook does not quite provide enough compensation for the sacrificed material.

White plays the mysterious Rook move **20. Ra1!.**

TAL: Quiet moves often make a stronger impression than a wild combination with heavy sacrifices.

Q: Doesn't this transgress the principle that Rooks belong on open files?

On the surface, yes. At this moment the Rook at a1 has no scope along the a-file. But the move has a fine defensive aspect in that it blunts Black's attack against b3, for 20 . . . axb3 21. axb3 opens the a-file for White's Rook. Sometimes you have to violate a principle to play the best move.

CHIGORIN: The best move today may be weaker tomorrow.

CONCEPT: Rooks should be placed along open files (files unoccupied by pawns), or on half-open files (files containing only enemy pawns), or on files that are likely to become clear of pawns through anticipated exchanges. They need scope in order to be effective.

CONCEPT: Violate any principle or rule of thumb if the position requires it. Principles are to be followed generally. They apply to most situations, not all. They are merely guidelines to direct the thinking process, nothing more. If you obey them absolutely, your game will collapse.

Black anticipates the opening of the a-file by **20 . . . Bb7.**

Q: Should Black so readily trade this Bishop?

Since Black is behind by a pawn, he should not rush to trade pieces. The more he does so, the greater the importance assumed by the extra material. If he plays 20 . . . Bc8, however, he encounters the debilitating 21. Bc6!, attacking the a-pawn and corraling Black's Bishop. Thus he decides that the Rook ending, with all its attendant pitfalls, offers greater defensive resources than an endgame with the Bishops still on the board.

White eats the Bishop **21. Bxb7.**

Q: Is keeping the Bishops on the board by 21. Bh3 better for White?

The shift 21. Bh3 assails the e-pawn, but Black holds with the useful 21 . . . Kf7. Besides, White has an extra pawn, and the correct plan when ahead is to trade pieces to accentuate the value of the extra pawn. With fewer pieces on the board, it becomes harder to develop counterplay and to stop the extra pawn if it gets past its enemy counterparts. Everything would then rest on the ability of the defending King to deal with what may be multiple threats.

CONCEPT: When ahead by a pawn, trade pieces, not pawns. When behind by a pawn, trade pawns, not pieces.

> **ALEKHINE**: It is obvious that every reduction of material will now be in White's favor.

Black takes the Bishop back **21 . . . Rxb7.**

Q: How does this Rook ending stand?

The key is that White has an extra pawn, which in most situations wins perforce. The idea is to create a passed pawn that will either become a new Queen or force the other side to make a significant concession in order to stop the pawn's promotion.

Comparing other factors, we see that Black's pawn structure is inferior to White's, especially on the Queenside where Black has three isolated pawns which cannot be protected by other pawns and therefore must be defended by pieces. Such defending pieces tend to become passive, one of the horrible things that can happen to them. A useful piece is one with scope, that can operate with relative ease. If you have weak pawns, the other side's King may be able to assume a powerful position in front of them on the squares that no pawn can guard. The final part of the puzzle is the Rook's position. Generally, you need your Rook to be active. Both players must be alert to opportunities to activate their Rooks.

White brings over his King by **22. Kf1.**

Q: What is White's plan?

It's to centralize his King and transport it to the Queenside where it can contribute to the defense of the Queenside pawns.

CONCEPT: As the endgame begins, centralize your King. The danger of it being attacked is not as great, and it can lend critical participation in the ensuing struggle. The King can guard important squares, support advances, and even help set up mating nets against its enemy counterpart. In the endgame, the King is a strong piece: use it.

LISITSYN: Decentralized Kings in the endgame are not well-placed, especially in the corner or at the edge of the board.

Black advances **22 . . . a5.**

Q: Why push this pawn?

If the a-file should open via an exchange of pawns, Black would have more opportunities for attack and defense with the pawn off the 7th rank. With the pawn at a5, Black could choose to place his Rook behind the pawn at a7 to protect it. Though this is not the best option, in some situations it could give Black a viable alternative. To confine the Black Rook to b7 for defense would be even more restrictive. Also, if the pawn is to be sacrificed to White's Rook, it's better to have White's Rook capture it without occupying the 7th rank, where there are more targets. Furthermore, by advancing the pawn, Black is trying to increase the chance of trading it for a healthy White pawn. Once Black's pawn is off the board, it never has to be defended again.

White inches along with **23. Ke1.**

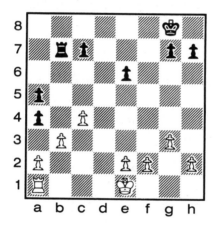

Q: Where does White hope to place his King?

On either c2 or c3, protecting his weakness and freeing his Rook for attack.

Black follows suit with **23 . . . Kf7.**

Q: What does this accomplish for Black?

It prepares to bring the King closer to the Queenside weaknesses, thus freeing the Rook from defense. It's more important for the Rook to be active than it is for the King. A passive Rook almost always leads to defeat in such endings.

CONCEPT: In the endgame, activate your Rook. Place it where it can easily spring into a defensive or aggressive position. An energized Rook can often offset positional and material liabilities. A passive Rook can lose you a game, sometimes even when you have material superiority.

White continues **24. Kd2.**

Q: After defending with his King, what is White's immediate plan?

To grab the d-file with his Rook. After a subsequent Rd1, White might flick his Rook to the 4th rank where it can shift to the Kingside to attack Black's pawns.

Black exchanges **24 . . . axb3.**

Q: What does this intimate about Black's intentions?

Black means to give up his a-pawn for White's b-pawn. If he doesn't do this now, White will station his King at c3, and Black will have forfeited his opportunity.

White takes back **25. axb3.**

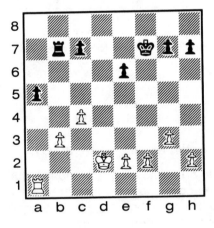

Q: *Instead of taking White's b-pawn, should Black play safe and guard his a-pawn by 25 . . . Ra7?*

This puts the a-pawn in a pin, subject to the predatory advance 26. b4. After the mandatory 26 . . . a4, White will be able to maneuver and eventually win the a-pawn by attacking it twice. The move 25 . . . Ra7 is also bad because it ties down Black's Rook to defense. It's essential for good defense in Rook endings to keep your Rook active.

Black plays **25 . . . Rxb3.**

Q: *In order to prevent 26 . . . Rb2 +, should White interpolate 26. Kc2?*

The check at b2 is not particularly meaningful, so why bother to stop it? White should stay with his plan and capture the pawn on a5.

CONCEPT: Don't engage in unnecessary or dilatory maneuvers. Don't prepare an action you can execute just as satisfactorily right away.

White remains a pawn ahead by **26. Rxa5.**

Q: *Does White have a threat?*

White threatens 27. Ra7, occupying the seventh rank and leading to the win of the c-pawn—it being in a pin and defenseless.

CONCEPT: Try to occupy the 7th rank with your Rooks. From there, the possibilities for winning material or giving mate are great.

Black inserts **26 . . . Rb2 +.**

Q: *Is this so helpful to Black?*

It in turn places the Black Rook on its 7th rank, poised to harass the enemy pawns. Though not essential, unless it's not played immediately, White will evaporate the chance by placing his King at c2.

White moves out of check **27. Kd3.**

Q: Which is better: 27. Kd3, 27. Kd1, or 27. Ke3?

The move 27. Kd3 is better. At e3, White's King blocks the e-pawn and doesn't defend the c-pawn. At d1, White's King is trapped on the back row, unable to participate in the proceedings.

Black defends with **27 . . . Ke7.**

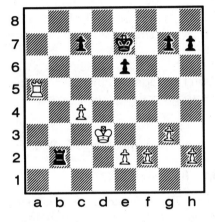

Q: What's the point of this?

It centralizes the King and answers the threat of 28. Ra7 with either 28 . . . Kd6 or 28 . . . Kd7.

White unleashes **28. h4!.**

Q: Why so?

On one hand, it gets the h-pawn off the 2nd rank, so it's less susceptible to enemy Rook attack. But more important, it eventually provokes a Kingside weakness after a subsequent h5, when White plans Rg5, attacking the g-pawn. This is part of the winning process: to create further weaknesses in the opposing camp.

Black gestures with **28 . . . Rb3+**.

Q: *Is this really a worthy check?*

Hardly. It's more of a time-gainer, just to see what White intends to do. If White, for example, plays his King to the 4th rank, Black can again occupy White's 2nd rank, compelling the King to retreat and waste time.

White foils this continuation with **29. Kc2**.

Q: *What does this force Black to do?*

He must snatch his Rook away from the 2nd rank, therefore securing White's pawns.

CONCEPT: Try to prevent the enemy Rook from penetrating behind the lines of your position. An active Rook-invader can wreak havoc.

Black guards his house with **29 . . . Rb7**.

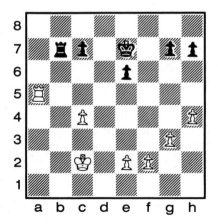

Q: Rook for Rook, how do White's and Black's compare?

Black's Rook has assumed a purely defensive role, guarding its 2nd rank. White's Rook is ready for action—along the 5th rank or the a-file. White's stands better.

CONCEPT: Try not to place your Rook in a purely defensive position. Its value will be greatly diminished.

White moves up **30. f3!.**

Q: How does this help White?

It gets the pawn off the 2nd rank, which is rather prone to a Rook invasion. Moreover, the move f3 is superior to f4 because it keeps e4 and g4 guarded by pawns. After 30. f4, White would relinquish pawn control of those two squares.

Black develops **30 . . . Kd6.**

Q: Why?

Surely to centralize the King and protect the weakness at c7.

White moves on with **31. h5.**

Q: What's the threat?

White is planning 32. Rg5. In order to defend his g-pawn, Black would have to accept further weaknesses by advancing his c-pawn. It's all part of the general scheme.

CONCEPT: If you are defending in the endgame, don't advance your pawns without specific purpose. Doing so would increase their organic weaknesses, making them more vulnerable. Advancing brings them closer to the other side's forces, exposing them to attack.

Black stops this with **31 . . . h6.**

Q: *This prevents 32. Rg5, but is it free from problems?*

On its negative side it weakens the square g6. Later this could be critical, especially if White's King can get to the weakened Kingside.

White penetrates with **32. Ra8.**

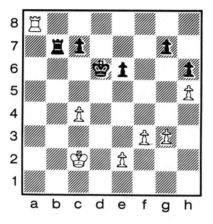

Q: *What does White plan?*

To attack the g-pawn, forcing Black finally to move up his c-pawn so that his Rook can provide protection.

CONCEPT: Try to penetrate the enemy front lines with Rooks so that they have access to the enemy weaknesses and targets.

CONCEPT: Try to induce your opponent to move his pawns and so create weak squares.

Black gives in by **32 . . . c6.**

Q: *Couldn't Black have waited a move before pushing his c-pawn?*

Yes, but doing it now gives him the sudden possibility of blocking checks with his Rook, should he need to. Unfortunately for Black, nothing can save his game at this point—certainly not trading Rooks.

White moves up with **33. Kc3.**

Q: Why does White play this?

To centralize his own King, in accordance with general principles and technique. Note the White King still maintains its hold over b2, preventing an enemy Rook incursion.

Black shifts to the Kingside **33 . . . Rf7.**

Q: How does this relate to White's 30th move, f3?

White anticipated such a possibility, a Rook attack to his f-pawn. If it had stayed at f2, it would now be under attack. Having dealt with this contingency earlier, White is free to continue uninterruptedly with his own plans.

CONCEPT: Try to anticipate future weak points in your position or attacks against you and prepare to counter them.

White continues **34. Kd4.**

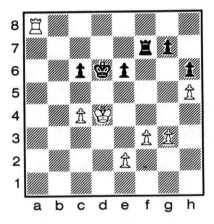

Q: *What does this demonstrate about the nature of the position?*

That White has the game completely under control. He has the time to improve the position of his King by bringing it to the center, where it will be prepared to play on either side of the board. Black must sit on his game and wait for White to undertake something, which is very hard for a defender to do.

CONCEPT: If there is no definite action to entertain, and if you have the time, strengthen your position before the final breakthrough.

Black reacts with **34 . . . e5 +**.

Q: *What is Black thinking of?*

Black fears that White would play 35. c5 +, leading to a trade of Rooks and a totally lost King-and-pawn endgame. Black's only hope is to keep his Rook to drum up counterplay.

White centers his King **35. Ke4.**

Q: *What is White's new target?*

After Black's last advance, White will focus on the e-pawn. The threat is 36. Re8.

Black forestalls the inevitable with **35 . . . Re7.**

Q: *Why does Black play this?*

To prevent 36. Re8, which would win the e-pawn.

White shifts to the 5th rank with **36. Ra5.**

Q: *What does this do to Black's position?*

It leaves Black in a kind of *zugzwang*, where he doesn't really have any good moves. If Black now moves his King, he loses his e-pawn. And if he moves his Rook along the e-file, he runs into the crushing 37. Ra7. Finally, 36 . . . c5 leads to 37. Ra6+ and 38. Kd5.

Black despairs with **36 . . . Rb7.**

Q: What does this move allow?

White can now take the e-pawn with his Rook.

Q: What will be the outcome of all this?

White will win a second pawn and have a triumphant position.

White's Rook takes the e-pawn **37. Rxe5,** leaving White two pawns to the good.

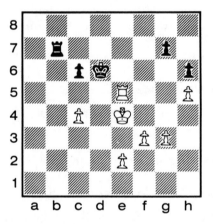

Black Resigns.

SMYSLOV: Not without reason did the great players from the past devote considerable attention to endings. In grasping the secrets of their mastery, I realized that the path to the heights of chess lies through an understanding of the laws of the endgame.

POSTSCRIPT

This game was distinguished by the consistent execution of a plan, drawn up as early as move 9:

  A) Saddle Black with weak pawns.
  B) Trade pieces.
  C) Contain all counterplay.
  D) Win in the endgame by exploiting the weak Black pawns.

White played the endgame very precisely. First he centralized his King so that it would be prepared for action and be able to guard certain squares. Then the Rook had to be activated so that it could exert its enormous powers against the Black bastions. White had to reduce possible counterplay by preventing the penetration of the Black Rook. In order to accentuate the strength of White's Rook, the Black Rook had to be tied down to defense. But even this wasn't sufficient. More weaknesses had to be induced so that White would have more targets—more ways to win material. White did not rush headlong into the attack, but built his position slowly and steadily until Black was reduced by total passivity. In the final stage, White used *zugzwang*—leaving Black without a reasonable move—which compelled Black to resign. White relied on brilliant position play against irreversible weaknesses.

BOTVINNIK: One of those games which have no pretty moves and therefore have the appearance of requiring no effort. Each move seems very simple and yet they are linked in a logical chain all the way. Such games are difficult to play, not because of their complexity, but because of the amount of time required to evaluate each move accurately.

Pawn Advances

WHITE: Gavrikov
BLACK: Cebalo
Vrsac 1985

WHAT TO LOOK FOR

Pawns play a starring role in this contest. Where, how, and when to move them is what this game is all about. The underlying fight pits White's center against Black's Queenside. Which carries more weight in the final analysis? This game shows the essence of contemporary pawn play, how it permeates the spirit of the entire game and how it forms the backbone of long-range planning.

PAWN MAJORITIES

Pawn majorities concern blocks of pawns of the same color (White or Black). You possess a pawn majority if, over any group of consecutive files, you have more pawns than your opponent. The three most described majorities occur on the Queenside, the Kingside, and in the center. The advantage of a healthy majority—one capable of moving satisfactorily—is that it gives you a greater chance to control that particular sector of the board. The disadvantage is that your opponent has superiority elsewhere, if the material is even. In that case, whoever can mobilize his majority more quickly and soundly tends to gain overall dominance.

CENTRAL INFLUENCE VS CENTRAL CONTROL

There are different ways to approach the center. You can occupy it, guard it, or influence it. In this game Black plans to influence the center by utilizing his Queenside majority to drive away White pieces that guard the center. Black's failure in this regard leads to his defeat.

RESTRAINT

This concept was first defined by Aron Nimzovich (1886–1935), who tied for first in the 1913 Russian championship. It concerns the process by which one tries to hinder an opponent from advancing specific pawns. When applied against healthy majorities, it prevents your adversary from realizing his potential. When used against an impaired pawn structure, it deters your opponent from ridding himself of stultifying weaknesses. Nimzovich believed the defender's whole game suffers when forced to defend weak pawns over the course of a game.

White moves out **1. d4.**

Q: *How quickly can this Queen-pawn opening transpose into a King-pawn opening?*

Next move. If Black, for example, plays 1 . . . e6, White can answer 2. e4 and create a French Defense. Or if Black essays 1 . . . g6, White can transpose into the Pirc-Modern Defense group also by 2. e4. The first move therefore does not always dictate the opening that follows. The initial play may simply reflect a move that's normally tried later on, made out of sequence.

CONCEPT: Play the first few moves very painstakingly. The course of the entire game is set early on. Move mechanically, and you may be stuck with a long-time disadvantage, impossible to overcome. Be alert from the start to set up a winning game.

Black responds **1 . . . Nf6.**

Q: *What's the key difference between 1 . . . Nf6 and 1 . . . g6?*

The move 1 . . . Nf6 prevents 2. e4. Otherwise, both replies for Black can lead to the same defenses. Black's actual first move stops White from transposing to a King-pawn opening.

White continues **2. c4.**

Q: *Can this still lead to a King-pawn opening?*

It can, in effect, but such a transposition is not likely or logical. From now on the opening should take on more and more Queen-pawn characteristics.

Some possible transpositions that can be arrived at through a different order of moves:

A) Caro-Kann Defense: 1. e4 c6 2. d4 d5 3. exd5 cxd5 4. c4 Nf6 5. Nc3 e6.
B) Queen's Gambit Declined: 1. d4 d5 2. c4 e6 3. Nc3 c5 4. e3 cxd4 5. exd4 Nf6.
C) Philidor's Defense: 1. e4 e5 2. Nf3 d6 3. d4 Nd7 4. c4 Ng-f6 5. Nc3 Be7.
D) Old Indian Defense: 1.d4 Nf6 2. c4 d6 3. Nc3 Nbd7 4. e4 e5 5. Nf3 Be7.

Black counters **2 . . . e6.**

Q: *Is Black's threatened check at b4 with his Bishop worth-while?*

What does it accomplish? Does it hinder White in some way or can White cope with it to his advantage? Perhaps White can even ignore it? In fact, the possibility of 3 . . . Bb4+ is not really a threat. If White were to play 3. Nf3, for example, the retort 3 . . . Bb4+ would be answered by 4. Bd2 or even 4. Nd2. The move 4. Bd2 probably results in a trade of Bishops and a weakening of Black's Kingside. Black's King-Bishop is more valuable to him than his opponent's Queen-Bishop is to White. Though the check at b4 is playable, it's not something to worry about. It merely signifies that Black has the opportunity of playing the Nimzo-Indian Defense (3. Nc3 Bb4). The contingency of pinning the Knight is greater than the possibility of issuing a check.

CONCEPT: Don't give automatic checks. As with any move, check only if it's a good move, and not for any other reason. An indiscriminate check may lose time and, sometimes, the game.

White builds with **3. Nf3.**

> **BOTVINNIK: Of course, the essence of chess is not to be found in the opening of the game. The basic ingredient of chess is that in a complex, original situation, where no source of help is apparent, a player must find the correct solution or move. Anyone who is able to do this can feel confident at the board.**

Q: Why does White choose to develop the King-Knight over the Queen-Knight?

White thus avoids the Nimzo-Indian Defense, which would follow after 3. Nc3 Bb4. The Nimzo-Indian would pressure White's center by pinning the Knight that guards the central squares e4 and d5.

CONCEPT: Look for indirect, subtle methods to accomplish your aims. It increases your chances of outplaying or swindling your opponent.

> **BRONSTEIN: When everything on the board is clear it can be so difficult to conceal your thoughts from your opponent.**

Black negotiates with **3 . . . c5.**

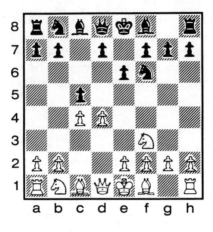

Q: What is the strategy of this move?

Black hopes to exchange an off-center pawn for a center pawn, thus creating for himself a central pawn majority. Black would then have a greater chance to control that region.

CONCEPT: Strive for central pawn majorities. They will enhance your ability to dominate the center and direct the flow of play.

White retaliates with **4. d5.**

Q: Why make this time-consuming advance?

White wants to evade the potential exchange of c-pawn for d-pawn. Advancing enables him to keep his central pawn. Moreover, at d5, White's pawn exerts a cramping stance over Black's position.

Black trades pawns with **4 . . . exd5.**

Q: What does this exchange indicate about the future layout of pawn majorities?

It means that Black will derive a pawn majority on the Queenside (have more pawns there than White) and White will derive a majority in the center. Black's attack will proceed from the Queen's flank while White's materializes in the middle. With all other factors equal, a central majority tends to be more important than a pawn advantage on the wing, though sometimes flank pawns can attack the center indirectly by dislodging enemy pieces controlling the central sector.

> **ALEKHINE: One of the most notorious prejudices of modern theory is that the Queenside majority is *in itself* considered an advantage, without any reference to whatever pawns or, more especially, pieces are concerned.**

CONCEPT: Use your wing pawns to dislodge enemy pieces defending the center. A well-timed flank advance can rattle a superficial defense.

White retakes **5. cxd5.**

Q: *What is White's eventual plan?*

White seeks the mobilization of his center. If successful, it will gain space, drive back enemy pieces, and produce a passed pawn, free to move up the board with the threat of becoming a new Queen.

White retakes **5. cxd5** and Black notches up with **5 . . . d6.**

Q: *How does this counter White's ultimate strategy?*

It releases the Queen-Bishop, which in some cases can be exchanged for White's Knight at f3, removing a support for the e-pawn's advance. Furthermore, at d6, Black's pawn adds protection to the crucial e5 square.

White strengthens his central grip with **6. Nc3.**

Q: *How does this mesh with White's plans?*

From c3, the Knight guards the salient squares d5 and e4, which must be secure if White's center is to become menacing.

Otherwise, Black's play against those squares will jeopardize White's envisioned thrusts.

Black flanks **6 . . . g6.**

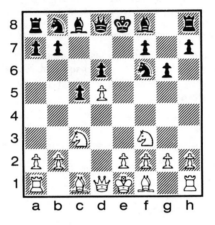

Q: Since Black has already moved his e-pawn, doesn't it waste time to now post his King-Bishop on the flank?

Not in this case. The Bishop's best placement is at g7. At e7, the Bishop's future is dim, for it has too little scope to assume more than a defensive role. From g7, it can reign supreme along the b2-g7 diagonal, for Black's Knight at f6 can be moved at his command. Granted, Black spends a bit more time completing his development this way, but his Bishop thereby augments its capabilities. Finding the best squares for your minor pieces is a typical leitmotif of the opening. Another question is: Do you have the right minor pieces for the position at hand? Correlating minor pieces with appropriate pawn structures is a particular skill of former world champion Anatoli Karpov.

CONCEPT: Don't just develop your minor pieces blindly. Make sure the squares you choose are the right ones, consistent with your overall plan. If you have the time, determine the most flexible placements and then develop the minor pieces.

CONCEPT: Try to exchange minor pieces so that you get the better of the deal—pieces more appropriate for the position at hand. For example, if the position is blocked, you might favor Knights. If it's wide open, you'd probably prefer Bishops.

White clears his Queenside back rank with **7. Bf4.**

Q: Is this consistent with White's game plan?

Yes. At f4, White's Bishop attacks the squares e5 and d6, lending general support to the planned central mobilization.

Black wings it with **7 . . . a6.**

Q: How does this fit in with Black's plans?

Black plans to advance his b-pawn to b5, protected by the a-pawn. If White doesn't counter, Black will advance one square further to b4, chasing away White's Queen-Knight, which guards the center. Here is a flank advance really aimed at the enemy center. Of course, 7 . . . a6 also prepares to mobilize Black's pawn majority.

CONCEPT: Use your advantages to mobilize your pawn majorities. Don't keep them in cold storage.

White meets Black head-on with **8. a4.**

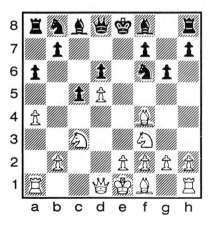

Q: Is this part of White's central plans?

Surely. White's advance stops the flank attack 8 . . . b5. Sans the ability to play this move, Black has to manufacture alternative, less effective methods to spray-gun White's center.

Black brings out his King-Bishop **8 . . . Bg7.**

Q: Can this Bishop contribute to the resistance to White's central advances?

Perhaps. At the necessary moment, Black's Bishop might add its weight to the defense of e5.

White King-pawns it **9. e4.**

Q: Is White threatening the immediate advance of the e-pawn?

At this point, the suggested pawn push would be premature, and certainly no threat. Black can confidently answer 10. e5 with 10 . . . dxe5, without imminent peril. White's resulting passed pawn would not yet be able to go anywhere, and he then has the added worry of having his own King caught in the center along the opened e-file. Such an advance must be better prepared.

CONCEPT: Timing is crucial. Don't execute desired actions unless the moment and attendant circumstances are right. Maximize the effect of your plans—if you have the time—before implementing them.

Black develops his Bishop by **9 . . . Bg4.**

Q: Does this move hint at Black's plans for this Bishop?

Black is implying that this Bishop may be less important than White's Knight. If it comes to it, Black will exchange minor pieces, reducing White's hold over e5. Black's development is thus designed to counter White's central plans. Besides, what other good squares does Black's light-square Bishop have? The choices are limited.

White prepares Kingside castling with **10. Be2.**

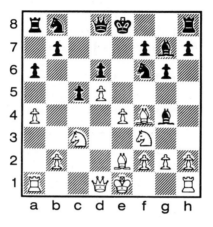

Q: Why develop the King-Bishop to e2 instead of d3?

At d3, the Bishop protects the e-pawn, but frustrates the Queen's future protection for the advance of the d-pawn, once Black's d-pawn is exchanged at e5. The Bishop from the d3 square may also face harassment by Black's c-pawn. After **10. Be2,** White's Bishop breaks the pin on the Knight at f3. This may give White the opportunity to save the Knight.

Black exchanges at once **10 . . . Bxf3.**

Q: Why this sudden exchange of Bishop for Knight?

If Black delays the exchange even one more move, White can opt for 11. Nd2, preserving this valuable steed. Later, the Knight can leap to c4, where it oversees e5 and d6, forming a vital link in White's plans.

White recaptures **11. Bxf3.**

Q: Doesn't the capture 11. gxf3 strengthen White's center?

For the meantime it protects e4 with another pawn. Generally pawn control is the safest and securest. Nevertheless, the doubled f-pawns would somewhat shred White's ability for future advances, and the weak squares on the Kingside and open g-file would discourage White from castling there. With his King stuck in the center, White's central prospects would be greatly reduced. More prudent is **11. Bxf3.**

Black clambers with **11 . . . Qe7.**

Q: Is this out of line with Black's defensive scheme?

No. At e7, Black's Queen overprotects e5, dissuading White from future advances. Black also wants to develop his Queen-Knight to d7, strengthening his grip on e5. To do so at once hangs the pawn at d6 to White's dark-square Bishop. The Queen at e7 means the d-pawn is no longer vulnerable to the Bishop at f4.

White castles **12. 0-0.**

Q: Why would White consider a move like 12. Qb3 instead of castling?

The move 12. Qb3 would deter 12 . . . Nb-d7, for that hangs the b-pawn to White's Queen.

Black follows through with **12 . . . Nb-d7.**

Q: Is Black's Knight heading for b6?

No. At b6 it blocks the Black b-pawn and exposes itself to the pesky pushing White a-pawn. Further, Nb6 is a diversion, not at all concerned with Black's plan of offsetting White's

---

KORCHNOI: Better to carry out a wrong plan logically than to play with no plan at all.

central advances. Such plan switches, without provocation, usually reap nothing.

CONCEPT: Don't change plans from move to move. Choose a suitable plan and continue it. Veer to another if you must or a more promising contingency suddenly materializes.

White centralizes with **13. Re1.**

Q: *How does this suit White's general plan?*

It supports the e-pawn now and for future advances. Black castles Kingside **13 . . . 0-0.**

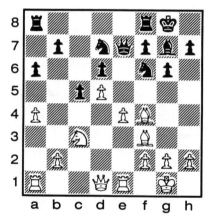

Q: *Why not castle Queenside instead?*

Queenside castling for Black would be extremely dangerous. If the center should then open, Black's King would be exposed to the full rays of White's Bishops. Moreover, with Black's King disposed to the Queenside, he couldn't push his flank pawns, which would only serve to open the position for his opponent. Black then would have to abandon his entire plan of attack. His play would be inconsistent.

White rises up with **14. Qd2.**

Q: What has this to do with White's goals?

Before undertaking action, White intends to complete his development. His pieces must first be deployed advantageously to secure the central marches. After this Queen's development, White is free to move his cornered Rook to the center. Such quiet preparatory moves are often undervalued and accordingly overlooked by many players. Also, **14. Qd2** gives White another chance to exchange dark-square Bishops at h6, a typical plan in similar situations.

Black Rooks up with **14 . . . Ra-b8.**

Q: Does this harmonize with Black's plan?

It's logical. Black heads for 15 . . . b5, hearing rumbles of a Queenside avalanche.

White repositions by **15. Be2!**

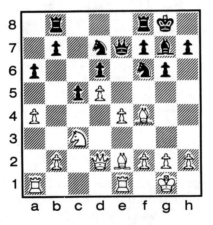

Q: What happens to White's e-pawn?

Nothing. If Black takes the pawn, 15 . . . Nxe4 16. Nxe4 Qxe4, he runs smack into the discovery 17. Bg4, uncovering an attack to Black's Queen from the Rook at e1 while also pinching the Knight at d7. For the odoriferous pawn Black would lose a piece.

Black Knights back with **15 . . . Ne8.**

Q: Why retreat the Black Knight?

Black plans to reposition the horse at c7, to bolster the push b5. The move also clears the dark-square Bishop's long diagonal. The Knight doesn't really retreat but maneuvers.

CONCEPT: Don't balk at temporarily retreating a piece if you intend to establish it in a better place. In certain conditions, such a piece is actually advancing backward! Taking one step back makes sense to go two steps ahead.

> **PETROV:** A retreat does not yet mean that the campaign is lost, for a defensive game may turn into an offensive one.

White sharply plays **16. Bg5!**

Q: Should Black answer this attack to his Queen by 16 . . . f6?

The defensive 16 . . . f6 saves the Queen, but also has at least two drawbacks:

A) It blocks the long diagonal of Black's Bishop.
B) It weakens the square e6 (no pawn control).

Black offers a trade with **16 . . . Bf6.**

Q: Should White now take advantage of the weakened dark squares and play 17. Bh6?

For White, this invasion leads nowhere. After 17. Bh6, Black can simply intercede with 17 . . . Bg7, still offering to trade Bishops and minimizing his weaknesses. Nor does repeating the position by then bringing the Bishop back to g5 seem to achieve clear results either.

White invigorates the position with **17. h4!?**

> **KASPAROV:** The disturbance of the equilibrium on all parts of the board promises a gripping struggle.

Q: *What does this do to White's pawns?*

After 17 . . . Bxg5 18. hxg5, White has doubled g-pawns. But Black has no definite method for attacking the pawns. Moreover, at g5, White's pawn attacks the inadequately protected dark squares, f6 and h6. Finally, with the h-file then open, White has a clear route to attack the Black King. One way would be to move up the g-pawn to g3, haul the King to g2, and then shift a Rook to h1.

CONCEPT: All other things being equal, avoid doubled pawns and other pawn weaknesses.

CONCEPT: Accept doubled pawns if they lead to other advantages that outweigh the pawn structure weakness. Remember that when doubled pawns are created via an exchange, an adjacent line is being opened. This clear channel may give you direct attack to the enemy King.

Black centers with **17 . . . Qe5?!**

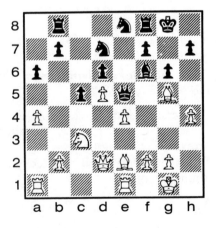

Q: Should Black have traded Bishops anyway, 17 . . . Bxg5?

Black could have played it that way, trading down Bishops, but he's hoping for more. Black wants to lure 18. f4, when he could swap down to an ending by 18 . . . Qd4+. In the endgame, Black needn't fear White's expansions. Even with the structural imbalances, White will have difficulty converting his transient advantage to victory.

White develops further with **18. Ra-d1.**

Q: What purposes guide this move?

White plays **18. Ra-d1,** desiring to centralize his pieces and generally prepare for pawn expansion. And lurking in the background is a hidden tactic that will soon be revealed.

CONCEPT: If preparing pawn advances, back them up with Rooks. As pawns move further up the board, the scope of the supportive Rooks increases.

> **PETROV:** Constant support has to be given to the central pawn.

Black pirouettes with **18 . . . Nc7.**

Q: Why does Black sally forth?

The move clears the back and places the Black Knight so that it protects the advance 19 . . . b5.

White deceives with **19. Qc1.**

Q: What does this move prepare?

White now menaces 20. f4, when Black's Rook at d1 prevents the Queen check at d4. This was the obscured tactical point to **18. Ra-d1.** Of course, the value of 20. f4 is that it supports the subsequent advance of White's e-pawn.

Black removes White's dark-square Bishop **19 . . . Bxg5.**

Q: *How should White back the Bishop, with his Queen or h-pawn?*

If White recaptures with his Queen, Black exchanges Queens with a chance to hold. If White takes back with the h-pawn, however, he retains chances to maybe trap Black's Queen. It's more sensible to take back with the h-pawn.

White answers **20. hxg5.**

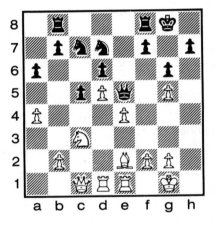

Q: *Can Black now begin his Queenside advances?*

Though the game may turn sharply quite soon, Black could start the pawns rolling with 20 . . . b5. That's his plan, and the faster he can satisfactorily inaugurate it, the better. When you try a radically different type of attack, such as a Queenside vault against an assault in the center, the more significant one tends to get there fastest. Your opponent won't even make the train.

CONCEPT: The best way to deter your opponent from attacking is to mount your own attack. Assail him first, and he'll not have time to launch his own initiative.

Black steps back by **20 . . . Qg7.**

Q: Why this play instead of the immediate b5?

Black anticipates the spiking 21. f4, knifing at his Queen. Rather than wait for that attack, he quickly deprives it of strength so he will have time for an extra defensive move if he needs it. Since the Queen must move after White's f4 anyway, Black is wasting no time at all.

White proceeds with **21. f4.**

Q: Should White change his plan and play for an eventual f5, shutting out Black's Queen?

This would be strictly a positional and tactical lemon. White's not really ready for a Kingside attack, and his best chances survive in the center, where he has a clear advantage. White's preparations have revolved around the push e5, and he lacks sufficient reason to change those plans. Consistency in such situations is crucial. Vary your ideas from move to move and you head nowhere.

Black retaliates with **21 . . . b5.**

Q: What two ways might this advance help Black?

On the one hand, it could lead in some circumstances to an opening of the b-file, after which Black's Rook and Queen converge on the b2 square. It also prepares a timely advance to b4, dislodging White's Knight at c3. The advance gives White something to ponder.

White lunges at Black's Knight with **22. Bg4!**

Q: Is this in agreement with White's plans?

Yes, in several ways. By threatening to capture the Knight, now or later, White would be removing a key defender of the square e5, facilitating the King-pawn's advance. The same

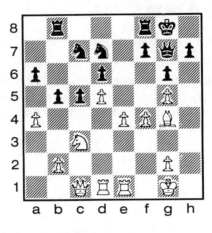

end would be achieved if, instead of being captured, the Knight moved to safety. Also, it makes sense to improve the scope of White's pieces before commencing the critical breakthrough. Everything must be just right. White's preparation is consistent.

Black defies White with **22 . . . f5.**

Q: Should White now play 23. exf5 or move his Bishop to safety?

Neither continuation is good. The exchange 23. exf5 gxf5 annihilates White's center, sapping him of all central juice. Without the King-pawn, no breakthrough is possible in the sector. And if White moves the Bishop to h3 or f3, Black also neutralizes the King-pawn with 23 . . . fxe4. Either of these proposed continuations, therefore, is inconsistent with White's aims.

CONCEPT: In many chess positions, it's not so important what your *next* move is, if it's reasonable. Critical, however, are the moves that follow. They must be logically consistent: All your moves should have their place in an overriding, integrated, coherent plan.

White captures *en passant* **23. gxf6.**

Q: How must Black recapture on f6?

Since 23 . . . Qxf6 hangs the Knight at d7 to White's Bishop, and 23 . . . Rxf6 allows 24. e5—because the Queen's control over e5 is then blocked—the only logical answer is 23 . . . Nxf6. It also has the virtue of attacking the Bishop, which may lead to a time gain if White has to waste a move to save the Bishop—unless the Bishop can do something that in turn gains time.

Black plays the imperative **23 . . . Nxf6.**

Q: How should White cope with the threat to his Bishop?

The most incisive answer is 24. Be6 + !. Positioning the Bishop radiantly in Black's camp and driving Black's King to the corner. After 24 . . . Kh8, White can finally push his pawn to e5. Black here can't exchange his Knight for the Bishop satisfactorily, as 24. Be6 + Nxe6 25. dxe6 gives White a powerful passed pawn and the opportunity to expose d6 to serious pressure.

White equivocates with **24. Bf3.**

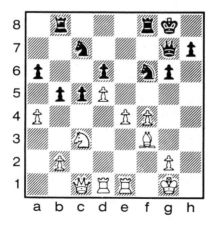

Q: What does this suggest about White's thinking?

Either that he imagines he has much better chances by keeping the Bishop on the board, or that he isn't quite sure of the consequences from 24. Be6+ and wants to play safely until the situation clears. Right or wrong, he prefers to maintain at least his slight advantage rather than risk it all on a move he's not sure about.

> **PETROSIAN:** As a rule in my games, when I have a choice between two continuations, one of which has unclear consequences (although instinct tells me that my chances will be more favorable) and the other leads to a clear and lasting advantage, I always prefer the clarity to complexity and risk.

CONCEPT: Mostly it's better to play a sure move that maintains a slight advantage over a risky one that evades clear judgment. Don't take unnecessary chances.

> **KARPOV:** Irrational play—going in for beautiful combinations and incalculable complications—can cost a point, even if only one out of ten. But I would rather win every one of the ten games with my technique. Today, for the sake of good results, the serious player often has to curb his desire to play beautifully.

Black regroups with **24 . . . Nd7.**

Q: How does this ally with Black's plans?

Again, Black is trying to grapple with the foreboding advance e5. By playing his Knight to d7, he adds a few protectors to e5: the Knight at d7 and the Queen.

White retrenches **25. Bg4!.**

Q: How does this increase White's potential?

White acquires the opportunity to trade Bishop for Knight, reducing Black's hold over e5. The trade might not happen immediately, but whenever White deems it correct and timely. The point is that White is now prepared for this exchange. Note how a light-square Bishop can fight for dark squares by attacking enemy pieces that guard them. White shows he will change his mind if he indeed sees a better idea.

CONCEPT: Don't be afraid to revise your thinking if you believe you've erred in judgment. Admit your mistakes and correct them. Make the best moves you can find, even if they seem to clash with your plans. Anyway, a good plan allows you to adapt to changing fortunes over the board.

CONCEPT: There's nothing wrong with repeating moves if they give you more time to consider a committal action. You should have some assurances before entering upon an irreversible path. Moreover, by repeating moves, your opponent may err or reveal something crucial about his understanding or intentions.

SHERESHEVSKY:(On the ability to sit on a position and not hurry moves) "Only in this way can a player achieve weakenings in the enemy position, mask his plans, and lull his opponent's vigilance." Shereshevsky adds that a cardinal factor with this principle is psychological. It may wear your opponent down. Of course, this idea of not hurrying applies more to static positions than to dynamic ones.

Black bolsters e5 with **25 . . . Rb-e8.**

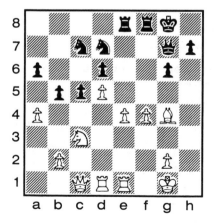

Q: *What does this mean about Black's Queenside demonstration?*

That it may come to naught, and that Black has decided mainly to deal with White's planned advance directly, by guarding the key square. He could have played 25 . . . b4, but after 26. Nb1, White will maneuver his Knight to c4 via d2. At c4 it is unassailable (no Black pawn can guard this square), and imperiously watches over e5 and d6.

CONCEPT: Certainly take a few moves to get your pieces to ideal squares, especially Knights, if the position affords you the necessary time.

White seizes the moment with **26. e5!**.

Q: *Does White's advance drop a pawn?*

This is a planned sacrifice to mobilize White's advantage. White reasons that what he will derive from the position in space and attack outweighs the temporary sacrifice of a pawn. The time has come for him to realize his central advantage— no further preparation is required.

Black takes the booty **26 . . . dxe5.**

Q: *Is it profitable to insert 26 . . . b4, driving away White's Knight, before capturing the e-pawn?*

The move 26 . . . b4 would be a mistake. It practically compels the Knight to occupy a commanding position at e4, overlooking c5, d6, f6, and g5.

> **SMYSLOV:** The Queenside stabilized, White is now ready for action on the other wing.

CONCEPT: Don't attack for attack's sake. In some cases, it may actually lead to improving your opponent's game.

White shoves ahead **27. d6.**

Q: Why does White advance this pawn?

It scatters and encumbers Black's forces even further. The breakthrough also opens up more lines for White's ready forces. As a rule, opening the position favors the attacker.

CONCEPT: If attacking, keep the game open. If defending, keep it closed.

Black focuses his Knight with **27 . . . Ne6.**

Q: Why not keep the e-file clear for Black's Rook by retreating the Knight instead to a8?

The Knight would be terribly out of things at a8. After a timely advance of White's Rook-pawn to a5, it wouldn't even have a safe move to get back in the game. Besides, it's needed for immediate heavy duty defense of the homeland.

White forges ahead with **28. Nd5!.**

Q: Does this threaten something concrete?

On the surface it menaces 29. Ne7+ as well as 29. Bxe6+ Rxe6 30. Nc7 Ref6 31. fxe5, with total positional superiority.

Black tightens up with **28 . . . c4.**

Q: How does this help Black's case?

It certifies Black's c-pawn is protected securely by another pawn, and it clears c5 for a Knight, if Black should want or need to move there.

White exchanges pawns **29. axb5.**

Q: Doesn't 29. Ne7+ win a piece (the Knight at e6)?

It doesn't win a full piece because Black can give up his Rook at e8 for the invading White Knight. After 29. Ne7+ Rxe7 30. dxe7 Qxe7, White's resulting material edge is too slight to guarantee a win in this position. The tactics in the situation are still complicated. So the move wins the exchange (a Rook for a Knight), not a full piece.

Black takes back **29 . . . axb5.**

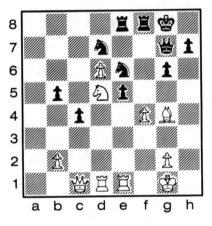

Q: *What do you think of the incursion 30. Nc7?*

After 30. Nc7 Nxc7 31. dxc7 Nb6, Black stops the c-pawn from Queening and may be able to organize a defense. The intrusion is not yet quite right.

White consumes the Knight **30. Bxe6 + !.**

Q: *Why does White down the Knight here?*

This possibility has existed for several moves. White opts for it now in order to play his own Knight to c7. Capturing the Knight on e6 removes c7's guard.

Black keeps the material balance with **30 . . . Rxe6.**

Q: *What can we say about Black's Queenside attack?*

It's been stopped. Both sides are now concerned solely with White's actions in the center.

White carries out his intention of **31. Nc7.**

Q: Should Black now sacrifice the exchange with Rf-e8?

No. After 31 . . . Rf-e8 32. Nxe8 Rxe8, Black doesn't really have enought for the lost exchange.

Black slides over with **31 . . . Re-f6.**

Q: Now what can we say about White's plan of centralized mobilization?

It has the look of success. White apparently can play 32. fxe5, creating connected passed pawns in the center. These pawns can move the board toward Queenland, undeterred by enemy pawns. Potentially, they're an awesome juggernaut, especially if supported from behind by well-posted Rooks.

> **BRONSTEIN:** Two passed pawns advancing on the enemy pieces have brought me more than a dozen points in tournaments.

CONCEPT: Try to create connected passed pawns. Enemy pawns can't stop them, and they can advance with protection from each other.

CONCEPT: Place Rooks behind passed pawns rather than in front. As a pawn advances up the board, the mobility of a Rook behind it increases while the mobility of a Rook in front of it decreases.

White establishes his center **32. fxe5.**

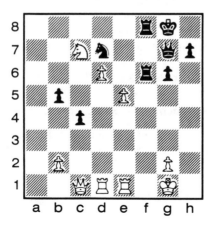

Q: *Where should the attacked Black Rook go?*

It can hardly go anywhere desirable. Whatever square the Rook moves to, White's devastating capacity to push the e-pawn with support clears away the Knight's blockade and prepares the march further. White's triumphant plan is almost complete.

Black last-ditches it with **32 . . . Nxe5.**

Q: *Why does Black sacrifice his Knight?*

What other practical way can he cope with the *putsch* of White's pawns? The sacrifice may work if Black can reach an endgame where, though he's behind by a Knight, the only pawns that remain on the board are on the Kingside: Black's two versus White's one. White's advantage might not be enough to force victory. Another drawing possibility arises if Black's Queen, in conjunction with a Rook, can harass White's King with checks and mate threats because of the sudden opening of lines in the center. To shelter his King, White might have to make concessions leading to a positional draw. Nevertheless, White will still be playing for a win, with very promising chances.

CONCEPT: Don't play resignedly if you have a losing game. Go down fighting. Your actual counterthreats and psychological resistance may prove too much for your opponent. He may experience a momentary letdown allowing you to save the game. Sometimes nothing is harder to win than a won game, and no one ever won by resigning. Soviet players—Karpov, Korchnoi, Botvinnik, *et al.*—exhibit a famed will power and mental toughness in the face of defeat.

White usurps the Knight **33. Rxe5.**

Q: *Can a Black tactic now win a pawn?*

Black can snatch White's d-pawn with his Rook, uncovering an attack to White's Rook from Black's Queen. Both sides would wind up losing a Rook—33 . . . Rxd6 34. Rxd6 Qxe5—but in the process Black wins the d-pawn.

Black follows through **33 . . . Rxd6.**

Q: *Instead of 34. Rxd6, what do you think of 34. Rc5, saving the Rook at e5 and defending the Knight?*

That fuels Black's counterattack after 34. Rc5 Rxd1 + 35. Qxd1 Qxb2, threatening 36 . . . Qf2 + and other nasty tribulations. White has no time to waste at this critical instant.

CONCEPT: Don't go out of your way to avoid one problem if it leads to even more serious difficulties. If you have the advantage, play simply, clearly, directly, making sure you maintain some of your advantage. Get through the complications and you should be all right.

White answers **34. Rxd6.**

Q: *Should White instead have played 34. Re-d5, doubling Rooks?*

Why ask for unnecessary trouble? Since White is ahead, he wants to simplify, not complicate. After 34. Re-d5 Rxd5 35. Nxd5, Black's Queen has a free move to begin aggressive action, such as 35 . . . Qa7 + or the centralizing 35 . . . Qe5. Get on with it.

Black crooks the Rook **34 . . . Qxe5.**

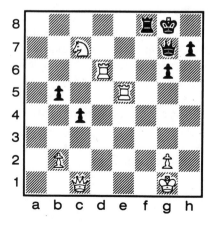

Q: *Should White now seize the 7th rank with his Rook 35. Rd7?*

White's invasion may look formidable, but it doesn't contend with Black's potential threats to White's King. After 35. Rd7 Qc5+, Black has at least a draw, since 36. Kh2 can be followed by 36 . . . Qh5+. White must deal with these checks if he is to win.

White protects his Rook with **35. Qd2!**.

Q: *Doesn't White's last move lose the Knight to 35 . . . Qc5+?*

White has looked a little further ahead than that. After 35 . . . Qc5+ 36. Qd4 (a powerful centralization) 36 . . . Qxc7 37. Rd7, Black must save his Queen and guard against the mate threat at g7. Note how White's Queen, posted in the center in this variation, shuts down all counterplay.

CONCEPT: In endgames with Queens, the best way to limit the opposing Queen's effectiveness is to centralize your own.

Black inertially plays **35 . . . Qc5+**.

Q: *Would Black have better chances by playing 35 . . . b4, trying to dissolve the Queenside pawns?*

No, because the Queenside pawns would not necessarily come off the board. White first trades Queens 36. Qd5+ Qxd5 37. Nxd5, and if Black continues 37 . . . c3, White keeps his b-pawn by 38. b3. The key is that 38 . . . Rc8 is not feasible because of the fork, 39. Ne7+. White should eventually win both Black Queenside pawns and retain his own b-pawn. That's a winning game.

White blocks the check **36. Qd4**.

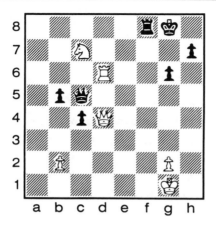

Q: *Can Black now avoid the Queen trade by 36 . . . Qb4,*
which may also threaten 37 . . . Qe1 + ?

Well, after 37 . . . Qe1 + 38. Kh2, Black doesn't have a
useful follow-up anyway. Meanwhile, White forces an immediate win with 37. Rd7 or 37. Ne6 or 37. Qd5 +. So Black
attempts one last desperate trick.

Black plays **36 . . . Rf5.**

Q: *What has inspired this Rook move?*

If White now trades Queens, which he generally wants to
do, Black's Rook takes back on c5, attacking the Knight and
backing up the advance of Black's c-pawn. Black thereby still
hopes to trade both of his Queenside pawns for White's b-
pawn, so that he has some drawing chances with his Kingside
pawn superiority. If eventually all the pawns come off the
board, the game would definitely be drawn, barring immediate tactics. A Rook and a Knight cannot ordinarily defeat a
lone Rook. No doubt about it, it's important to retain some
pawns in so-called won endgames.

CONCEPT: If you have an extra minor piece in the endgame, don't trade off all your pawns. The extra piece may not
be enough to win without the additional aid of promoting a

pawn. Try to keep at least a couple of pawns so that you can threaten to make a new Queen.

White invades **37. Rd8 +** .

Q: If White intends to occupy the 7th rank with his Rook, why doesn't he simply move there at once 37. Rd7?

An immediate move there loses a move, for Black can then trade Queens, forcing White's Rook to back off the 7th rank. By starting with this checking invasion, White can check his way to the 7th rank, and black never gets the opportunity to play a timely trade.

CONCEPT: If you can achieve the same effect with either a checking or a non-checking move, by all means play the check. Since the checks force your opponent's responses, he won't have as many surprise opportunities to upset your plans. He's got to get out of check first. Checking facilitates your keeping control of the situation.

Black flees **37 . . . Kf7.**

Q: What about 38. Rd5? Wouldn't that now force some more trades?

It's true that 38 . . . Qxc7 is not good because of 39. Rd7 +, but Black still has 38 . . . Qxd4 39. Rxd4 Rc5, with improved opportunities over previous lines. The move 38. Rd5 is too slow and blunderous.

White occupies the 7th rank with a gain of time **38. Rd7 +** .

Q: Is Black's response to this move forced?

Yes, for 38 . . . Kf8 loses the Queen to the Knight fork 39. Ne6 +. Black has only one move.

Black plays the inevitable **38 . . . Kg8.**

Q: *Does White now force a win with 39. Ne6?*

It's a bit murky after 39 . . . Qxd4 40. Nxd4 Rc5.

White resolves the issue with **39. Nxb5!**.

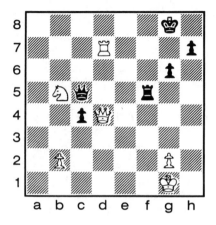

Q: *Why does this work?*

Black is unable to take the Knight, 39 . . . Qxb5, because of 40. Qg7 mate. On the other hand, after trading Queens, Black's c-pawn poses no serious threat. White will keep his b-pawn and eventually win the pawn at c4 and the game.
Black Resigns.

POSTSCRIPT

This game exemplified strategy based on pawn structure. Two opposing plans confronted each other in a battle of pawn majorities. Ultimately, White's central majority proved stronger than Black's Queenside majority—in this game.

Black's Queenside mobilization developed accordingly. He prepared the advance of the b-pawn with **7 . . . a6, 14 . . . Ra-b8,** and **18 . . . Nc7.** White tried to frustrate in turn. The moves **6. Nc3, 8. a4,** and **15. Be2!** all dealt with Black's Queenside advances.

White's central plan needed its own preparation. The ideas **18. Re1, 15. Be2!,** and **16. Bg5!** (the latter two moves clearing the f-pawn's path), **18. Ra-d1,** and **19. Qc1** were all concerned with the success of this campaign.

Black restrained these advances with direct counterpunches. The move e4-e5 was detained because of **9 . . . Bg4** and **10 . . . Bxf3.** This transaction removed an important guard for e5. Black also overprotected e5 by **5 . . . d6, 11 . . . Qe7, 12 . . . Nb-d7,** and **15 . . . Ne8,** opening the dark-square Bishop's diagonal.

Black hoped to brand White's e-pawn, ultimately, as a weakness. His plan was to immobilize the pawn at e4 by controlling e5. Then he had hoped to attack the e-pawn with heavy pieces (Rooks and Queen) along the e-file. He would follow with a timely b5-b4, driving away a key protector of e4, the Knight at c3. To undermine the whole center, he would have, as a last resort, the thrust f5. In a sense, the Black play on the Queenside is secondary to the main operation, the attack against e4. Black's Queenside advances are to be viewed as guerrilla war tactics to divert the enemy from his own aims.

The critical moment in the game arose when White played **26. e5!,** in the teeth of Black's control over that square. Great accuracy in calculation was needed to justify this sacrifice. The culminating moves, **27. d6** and **28. Nd5,** typical follow-ups in similar situations, proved White correct. He emerged with the positional superiority required to win. The rest was technique. A beautifully conducted game. A precisely executed march of central pawns.

LESSON 5

Counterattack and Tactics

WHITE: Panczyk
BLACK: Yusupov
Warsaw 1985

WHAT TO LOOK FOR

The key to this game is tactics. The swordplay is touchy, fraught with traps and tricky variations, but Black's is a more soundly based attack. His operation stems from a position of greater strength, embodied in greater piece development. In the end, Artur Yusupov, one of the world's leading grandmasters, sees more deeply, clearly, and accurately into the position. He's living proof of how quickly the hunted can become the hunter.

WHITE'S KINGSIDE ATTACK

White piles his stakes on a Kingside attack. Relying on greater apparent force in the area, setting traps to lure away defenders, White hopes to denude Black's King coverage and deliver a knockout. But his lagging development causes him to lose valuable time defending his position and leads to dissipation of the initiative.

BLACK'S COUNTERATTACK

Black seems defensive at first, and indeed is. But White's attack is premature. Instead of building his assault naturally, with gradual development, White tries to rally his forces before they're ready for it. He's repulsed because he really has no advantage. Black waits until White overextends himself. Breaking the assault with a precisely calculated sacrifice, he exploits his opponent's lack of harmony. Employing a dangerous passed pawn, he gains material and wins in the endgame.

PASSED PAWN

A *passed pawn* is one that is free to move up the board, unhindered by opposing pawns, either in front or on adjacent files. Black's incisive counterattack produces a dangerous passer that diverts White from his own offensive and leads to a winning promotion. Black's Queen and Rook play an active part in paddling home the win.

White opens up with **1. d4.**

Q: *How does this move weaken White's King's position?*

It exposes His Majesty to attack along the e1-a5 diagonal. Curious ways to exploit this may emerge if White isn't circumspect. A popular trap arises from the Cambridge Springs Variation of the Queen's Gambit: 1. d4 d5 2. c4 e6 3. Nc3 Nf6 4. Bg5 Nb-d7 5. cxd5 exd5 6. Nxd5 (trying to capitalize on the pinned Knight) 6 . . . Nxd5! 7. Bxd8 Bb4+ 8.Qd2 (forced) 8 . . . Bxd2+ g. Kxd2 Kxd8, after which Black is a piece for a pawn ahead. Of course, White's first move is not really weak, but it's important to realize that practically every move, good or bad, has two sides.

CONCEPT: Whether considering a move, a variation, or a plan, be sure to evaluate in depth, balancing the positive against the negative. Only then, after you've examined both sides of the coin, can you decide if your ideas are right.

POLUGAEVSKY: At times a chessplayer cannot get by merely by working out moves and continuations. Just as an artist painting a picture should from time to time break off from making individual brush strokes, and, taking a step back, take in the complete canvass at a glance, so too a chessplayer, by simply resorting to an abstract approach, is able as if from the side to assess his ideas and calculations, examine the impasse lying in wait for him, and find that turn which is able to lead the position out onto the highway of chess practice.

Black counters 1 . . . **Nf6.**

Q: *How do you feel about 2. Bg5, threatening to capture on f6, disrupting Black's pawn structure?*

Black has plenty of ways to answer the threat. With the move 2. Bg5, White hopes Black will permit his Knight to be pinned by moving the pawn to e6. Since no pin exists on the Knight yet, Black can switch circumstances by 2 . . . Ne4. Instead of being pinned, the Knight moves out to attack the Bishop. Early Bishop attacks against Knights can often lead to role reversals.

CONCEPT: Don't automatically develop Bishops in anticipation of pins to Knights. You may lose the initiative if your opponent avoids the pin and moves to charge the Knight against the Bishop.

White expands with **2. c4.**

Q: *What about the alternative, 2. c3? Is it much different from the move actually played?*

The thrust 2. c4 is more aggressive. It attacks the center at d5, and gives White more space. From c4, White's c-pawn supports central advances, along with the Queen-Knight if it moves to c3. If the move were 2. c3, however, the Queen-Knight must be developed elsewhere. And though the solid 2. c3 protects

White's d-pawn, it's rather passive. Preparing for the attack with **2. c4** makes more sense.

> **KASPAROV: Dynamic positions demand bold decisions on every move and an alternation of strong and solid moves does not produce good results.**

CONCEPT: If you have the choice between attack and defense, attack. The defender is at a very great disadvantage, having to haunch back and wait for play to develop. Better to control the action yourself so at least you know what's coming.

Black clears the King-Bishop's diagonal by **2 . . . e6.**

Q: How might the game develop if Black opts to flank his Bishop by 2 . . . g6 instead?

Usually chess games, from the position created by the actual move, flow in two well-charted directions. Black could flank his Bishop at once, setting up the King's Indian Defense by 3. Nc3 Bg7 4. e4. White gets a pawn center and play on the Queenside, as Black musters pressure against the center and on the Kingside. Or Black could delay completing the flank by continuing with the Gruenfeld Defense, 3. Nc3 d5. Here, Black hopes White mishandles his central pawn mass, abandoning the region eventually to Black. Both lead to sharp, complex positions, the calling card of the "young Turk" Russians.

> **KASPAROV: The classical approach to chess, which assigns Black the role of the defending side in the opening, sets him the immediate task of equalizing. But progressive chess thinking was unable to reconcile itself to such an approach to the problems of the opening. There are now a number of systems in which Black encroaches upon White's privilege in the opening—the right to the obtaining of an advantage.**

White develops **3. Nc3.**

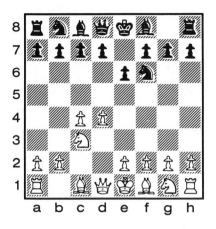

Q: *Does White have a threat?*

If Black plays indifferently, White will enlarge his center with 4. e4. One way to stop White's proposed advance is with the head-on 3 . . . d5. Another way is black's actual third move.

Black sets up the Nimzo-Indian Defense with **3 . . . Bb4.**

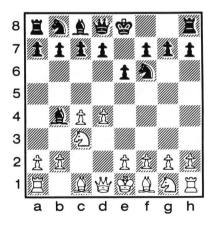

Q: How does this cope with White's plan?

By pinning the Knight at c3, Black deprives White of support for advancing the e-pawn. Black's strategy relies on pieces to restrain White's center pawns. So far, Black's Knight and Nimzo-Bishop do the job. One asset of the Nimzo-Indian is psychological—it keeps White guessing as to how Black will ultimately use his center pawns. That Black hasn't moved his d-pawn two squares ahead yet doesn't mean he never will.

White plays **4. e3.**

Q: Should White fear the exchange on c3, doubling his pawns?

No. After the exchanges 4 . . . Bxc3 + 5. bxc3, White is left with doubled c-pawns, but with several compensating advantages. For one, he has two Bishops to Black's one because of the exchange on c3. Early on, it's generally desirable to have Bishops, which ordinarily rank more useful than Knights. White moreover will have superior chances in the center, thanks to his preponderance of pawns there. Helpful would be the b-pawn coming to the center at c3, where it's a valuable addition to White's middle. The doubled pawns are not really so weak unless they become blocked and immobilized. If White can exchange one of them, he'll no longer have doubled pawns, and circumstances change.

CONCEPT: Play for the "two Bishops," which is having two Bishops against a Bishop and Knight or against two Knights. Most times the dome-headed duo works as a real advantage.

CONCEPT: Don't worry too much about avoiding doubled pawns in the opening. The more important battle in the early stages hinges on controlling the initiative: on being better developed, having more space, superior use of open lines, greater King safety—being able to direct the flow of play. Certainly avoid them if you can do so naturally, as an outgrowth of your game, but if you focus too much on positional considerations you may get checkmated.

Black swoops into the center with **4 . . . c5.**

Q: *What is Black's main reason for playing this?*

He wants to pressure White's d-pawn. If White winds up exchanging at c5, he surrenders the center. If he pushes to d5, in some situations his center becomes dead wood and vulnerable to attack, especially if an exchange occurs on c3. An added feature of 4 . . . c5 is that it opens a diagonal for Black's Queen to the Queenside.

White builds in the center with **5. Bd3.**

Q: *What thematic plan could White now follow to control e4?*

White plans to marshal his center pawns. His Bishop now controls e4 from d3. White could develop his King-Knight to f3, but to influence e4 he could play his Knight to e2, keeping the f-pawn unblocked. It may be needed at f3 to control e4. At e2, furthermore, the Knight is ready to hop to g3, which also controls e4. Later White's Queen-Rook might assume the e-file for backup, and the Queen could reside on c2 or e2. These are all plausible placements.

CONCEPT: Think of opening schemes. When developing a particular piece, try to envision where your other pieces might go afterward. How does one development affect the others? Trying to imagine how the pieces will work together ahead of time is the best way to achieve a harmonious setup. Otherwise, you may wind up stepping on your own toes.

Black resumes his central action with **5 . . . Nc6.**

Q: *Is this consistent with his previous play?*

As with his previous move, Black is asserting his interest against d4. If the pressure intensifies, White may be lured into a mistake or an overreaction.

White chooses the thematic move **6. Ne2.**

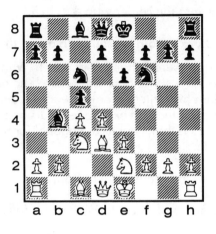

Q: What does this move do?

It swings many arms (like Krishna?). It develops a piece toward the center, protects the Knight at c3, prepares castling, and positions the Knight to be shifted to g3, as in a previous discussion. In some situations the Knight could also go to f4, especially to focus on the square d5. White's Knights protecting each other makes it possible to avoid doubled pawns on c3. On 6 . . . Bxc3 +, White has the option to play 7. Nxc3.

Black initiates an exchange by **6 . . . cxd4.**

Q: What does Black have in mind?

The transaction allows Black to exchange an off-center pawn for a center pawn, giving Black a central majority. In some instances, it also gives Black's dark-square Bishop a retreat along the a3-f8 diagonal.

White takes back **7. exd4.**

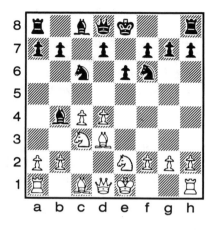

Q: Would 7. Nxd4 be a better way to recapture?

The Knight capture is surely playable. It might make special sense if White had a way to exploit the square d6 after subsequently moving the Knight to b5. This is not likely, though the Knight capture is possible. If the Knight capture has any drawbacks it's that 7 . . . Bxc3 + 8. bxc3 inflicts White with doubled isolated pawns, which can be worse than ordinary doubled pawns because neither isolated doubled pawn can be protected by another pawn. A secondary problem with the Knight capture on d4 is that it keeps a pawn at e3, blocking the diagonal of White's dark-square Bishop.

CONCEPT: Release undeveloped Bishops by moving obstructing pawns out of their way as soon as possible.

Black lands on the beach with **7 . . . d5.**

Q: What does this advance do?

It gives Black a share of the center by establishing the d-pawn right there. In some cases, Black could exchange pawns to isolate White's d-pawn, forcing White's pieces to keep it defended. Should White accept an isolated d-pawn, he will find his Knight not so well placed at e2, where it's burdened with a primarily defensive task. It would be better instead to keep it at f3, still shouldering the d-pawn but also glowering at e5—a great outpost square for a Knight. A seat on the 5th rank, protected by a pawn, can elevate a Knight to great heights.

CONCEPT: Try to establish Knights in outpost squares, entrenched in the enemy camp on the 5th and 6th ranks, protected by friendly pawns, and unassailable to enemy pawn attacks.

White breezes along with **8.0-0.**

Q: Should White instead have exchanged pawns 8. cxd5?

If White wants to accept the isolated d-pawn, this is not the best way to do it. After 8. cxd5 Nxd5, Black has posted his Knight powerfully in front of the weak d-pawn, creating a "blockade," (when an opposing piece can capitalize on the weak square in front of an isolated pawn by occupying it). The piece can sit there because the isolated pawn has no adjacent pal to drive such pieces away. Better to have Black isolate the pawn by 8 . . . dxc4 9. Bxc4, when White's Bishop at least slides to a more aggressive square, asserting itself against the weak d5.

CONCEPT: Try to blockade an enemy's isolated pawn by placing an effective piece, such as a Knight, in front of it.

CONCEPT: Prevent your opponent from blockading your own isolated pawn. If you can't, try to slow up the process.

White castles, **8. 0-0,** and Black goes to market, **8 . . . dxc4.**

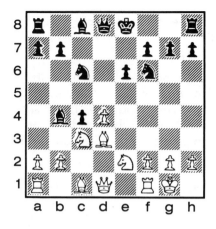

Q: *What is Black's plan?*

It's to:

- Isolate White's d-pawn.
- Prevent it from moving by guarding the square in front of it.
- Attack it with pieces, such as a Knight from c6, a Bishop from b6, and a Rook along the d-file.
- Force White into a passive position.
- Constrain White to make positional concessions.
- Win the pawn.
- Trade down to reach an endgame.
- Convert the extra pawn into a win, either by gaining more material or making a new Queen.

White regains his pawn with **9. Bxc4.**

Q: *What is White's plan?*

It's to:

- Take advantage of the open lines.
- Occupy e5, preferably with a Knight.
- Develop Kingside attacking chances.
- Advance his pawn to d5, exchanging it for Black's e-pawn.

Black castles **9 . . . 0-0.**

Q: *If White succeeds in advancing his pawn to d5, exchanging it for Black's e-pawn, what advantage will he have?*

Centralization. After exchanging on d5, regardless how many items are exchanged, White will be the last to capture on that square. He will therefore have a piece amidst the fray after the transaction, which may give him a slight initiative. It depends how opportunely White pushes the pawn, for he must have enough protection on d5 before this becomes feasible.

CONCEPT: Try to control the square in front of your isolated pawn. If you can successfully exchange the pawn by advancing, it should give you a slight spatial advantage.

White attacks the Bishop with **10. a3.**

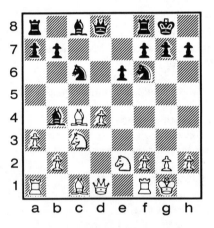

Q: *What's the purpose of this?*

White wants to stabilize things. He's banking that either the pressure on the Knight will be abated or Black will exchange Bishop for Knight, solidifying White's center and giving White the "two Bishops." The liabilities are a minimal weakening of the light squares (b3) and a waste of a tempo that could have been used to develop a new piece.

CONCEPT: To clarify the circumstances of a Knight on its Bishop-three square (c3 here) attacked by a Bishop on its Knight-five square (b4 here), consider attacking the Bishop by moving the Rook-pawn one square. First, however, be sure the advance does not damage your position by creating irreparable weaknesses.

Black takes the Knight **10 . . . Bxc3.**

Q: Should White take back with Knight or pawn?

It's convenient if White could capture with his Knight 11. Nxc3, for that brings another piece to bear on d5. This is in line with the plan of guarding the square in front of the isolated pawn before pushing it. But 11. Nxc3 loses the d-pawn, for Black then has two attackers beamed on it—the Queen and the Knight at c6—against White's lone protector, the Queen. White really has no choice—he must retake with the pawn 11 bxc3.

CONCEPT: In order to win an enemy pawn through direct capture, generally you must have more pieces attacking it than are defending it—you must be able to capture last. The chief exception arises when the attacking units are of superior quality to the protectors. For example, if you have two Knights assailing a pawn that is protected by a lone pawn, capturing with either Knight would lose material—it being significantly more valuable than the opposing pawns.

White completes the transaction with **11. bxc3.**

Q: How do you evaluate the present pawn structure?

White's d-pawn has been strengthened by this last capture. It's now guarded by the c-pawn, which used to be the b-pawn. White's pawns, however, exist in three groups:

1) On the a-file.
2 On the c- and d-files.
3) On the f-, g-, and h-files.

Black's pawns are laid out in just two groups:

1) On the a- and b-files.
2) On the e-, f-, g-, and h-files.

It's usually desirable to have as few pawn groups or "islands" as possible, for it's then easier to defend them. In the endgame, White's isolated a-pawn might become a target for Black's pieces. Much depends on what White can now do with his central block of pawns. If later he can advance his c-pawn to c4, his c- and d-pawns together will guard a line of key central squares, from b5 to e5. Each pawn, if reasonable, could support the other's advance. Yet these pawns face considerable attack too, by virtue of simply being out there on the 4th rank. And if Black can totally restrain the c-pawn's movement, White may wind up being cramped, without any real compensating dynamism.

Pawns aligned on the 4th rank of the c- and d-files, which are strong when they can successfully advance and weak when they come under heavy piece attack—especially from enemy Rooks along half-open files in front of them—are called *hanging pawns*. Like isolated d-pawns, they can be good or bad depending on the prevailing circumstances of the position.

Pawns held back at c3 and d4 (or in comparable placements elsewhere) by enemy pawns on adjacent files and subject to enemy piece aggression are known as the *isolated pawn pair*. Often the enemy's pieces can immunely occupy the squares immediately in front of the pawns, for no opposing pawns can drive the pieces away. Even though the pawns are on adjoining files, they suffer from the same afflictions of isolated pawns, especially when the opponent dominates the squares in front of them. Such pawns tend to provide little, if any, compensation to their owner.

CONCEPT: Avoid accepting the isolated pawn pair. It usually leads to a passive game, with virtually no compensation.

CONCEPT: If you have an isolated pawn pair, try to align both pawns safely on the 4th rank, creating a hanging pawn pair (hanging because temporarily neither pawn protects the other), increasing the tension and potential in the position. The advantages you get may outweigh the liabilities.

Black safeguards with **11 . . . h6.**

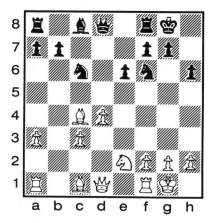

Q: Why does Black risk this pawn move?

Generally, you shouldn't move the pawns in front of your King in an open game unless you must or you have a definite purpose. Moving such pawns weakens squares around your King and gives your opponent potential targets as you bring your pawns closer to his forces. Black reasons here, however, that it's wise to stop White's Bishop from going to g5, pinning Black's f6 Knight. Such a pin might prove more deleterious for Black than this advance's accompanying weakness.

CONCEPT: When the center is open, don't move the pawns in front of your castled King unless for a specific purpose. Ill-considered advances can provide your opponent with precarious targets that corrode your entire game.

CONCEPT: Look for targets and weaknesses in your opponent's camp and focus your attack against them.

White trots over to the 4th rank **12. Nf4.**

Q: *Why station the horse here?*

From f4 it supports a subsequent advance of the d-pawn and also overlooks h5, to which it might swagger to inspirit a Kingside attack. A rarer possibility is the transfer to d3, and later to e5. A more precise development would have been 12. Bf4, bringing out a new piece and overprotecting e5—a square Black needs to control if his e-pawn is to advance.

CONCEPT: If you determine a strong possible placement for a Knight, but are unable to move it there directly, think backward. Focusing on the target square, imagine moving in the other direction toward the starting square, as you would try to solve a maze (you work backward until you reach a point that can be seen from the start). This is a helpful technique to improve your receptivity for Knight maneuvers.

Black unblocks the back row with **12 . . . Bd7.**

Q. *How would White have answered the thrust 12 . . . e5?*

White could have continued 13. Ng6!, when the pinned f-pawn is unable to guard g6. This surprising tactic allows White to maintain the tension of the position and dissuades Black from this natural freeing move.

White relocates his Bishop, **13. Ba2.**

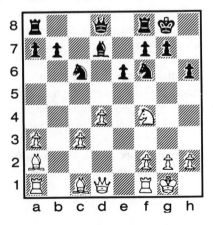

Q: *How does this move fit White's plans?*

Two ways. At c4, the Bishop is vulnerable to attack—by either a Rook or Queen along the c-file or by a Knight from a5. To cope with this threat White later may have to waste time. And by withdrawing the Bishop, White clears the path of his c-pawn so it can move to the 4th rank, achieving favorable hanging pawns.

Black volleys **13 . . . Rc8.**

Q: *Why swing the Rook to this file?*

Rooks should be placed on open files (files with no friendly pawns in the way). They then have an unobscured view of the enemy embankments. While Black's c6 Knight is temporarily obstructing the Rook's vision, it can be moved conveniently aside (say, Na5) uncovering a threat to White's c-pawn. The Rook's move is a typical position builder.

CONCEPT: In addition to firing immediate attacks, look for possible future threats. Ask yourself questions that ferret out information about the position. This is a helpful process in formulating a plan.

White patrols the open file with **14. Re1.**

Q: *Why take the open file now?*

Defensively, White wants to prevent Black from striking back with 14 . . . e5. Offensively, White is mulling a Kingside attack, following up with 15. Re3 and transferring the Rook along the 3rd rank to the Kingside. A better play for White, however, is 14. d5. After the obligatory 14 . . . exd5 15. Nxd5, the game should be about equal. White will have centralization and the two Bishops against Black's slightly better development and play against the isolated c-pawn. But White mistakenly thinks he can get more by restraining Black's e-pawn and averting exchanges.

CONCEPT: Don't force the situation. If you feel you have nothing better than a draw, accept the consequences. Should you overextend yourself trying to win, the counterattack may kill you.

POLUGAEVSKY: I am not an advocate of brilliance for brilliance's sake, if there exists a more rational possibility.

Black resumes with **14 . . . Re8.**

Q: With what idea?

Black plans to continue with the anticipated advance e5. And if White insists on pushing the d-pawn, the resulting exchanges will suitably place Black's Rook on the then open e-file.

White plunges ahead recklessly with **15. Re3.**

Q: Instead of this Rook shift, what else could White do?

Among several options, White could have developed his Queen-Bishop, say to b2, hoping to push his c-pawn; or he could have played even more tactically with 15. Qf3, discouraging 15 . . . e5 because of 16. Nd5, with tricky complications. White's problem is that since his Queen-Bishop is undeveloped, his back rank can become potentially weak.

CONCEPT: Before committing yourself to a full-scale attack, be sure your pieces are developed enough and that you have no glaring weaknesses. Otherwise, your rampage may screech to a halt, defending against a timely threat, and you might not be able to recover.

RUSSIAN SAYING: One man in a field is not an army.

Black confronts White with **15 . . . e5!**.

Q: Should Black instead have tried to occupy d5 with a Knight by preparing it with 15 . . . Ne7?

That repositioning here is too slow and fruitless. After 15 . . . Ne7 16. c4!, the unclear nature of the position might favor White with his two Bishops, expanding pawns, and open lines. Black must blunt White's frenzy now.

The attack proceeds with **16. Nh5!**.

Q: What's happening here?

The position has suddenly reached a crisis where irreversible things are looming. Some possibilities:

• Black could attack the Rook and prepare the entrance of his Queen: 14 . . . Ng4 17. Rg3 Qh4 18. h3, and White should get the better of it.

- Black could trade Knights: After 16 . . . Nxh5 17. Qxh5, White has intense Kingside pressure.
- Black could coolly ignore the threat and continue as in the game.

With considerable sang-froid, Black takes a pawn **16 . . . exd4!.**

Q: Should White first play the in-between move 17. Nxf6 + ?

This would merely help Black's game. After 17. Nxf6 + Qxf6 18. Rf3, Black has the *zwischenzug* (in-between move) 18 . . . Bg4!, eviscerating White's blitz and arriving ultimately at a position favoring Black. White's attack would come to zero, sounding fury and nothing else.

CONCEPT: Before playing out a combination or sequence of practically forced attacking moves that you've mentally worked out, check if your opponent has any surprise moves that could create a snafu. A sudden enemy check or threat (such as the pin 18 . . . Bg4! in the above analysis) could disrupt the entire variation.

White plays for a trap with **17. Rg3.**

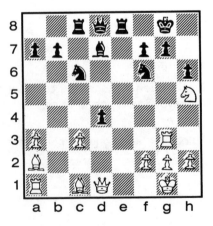

Q: Can Black undo it with 17 . . . Nxh5?

No, it allows the trap. After 17 . . . Nxh5, White doesn't follow with 18. Qxh5, but instead has the *zwischenzug* 18. Bxf7 + !. There are three plausible variations from there:

1) Black could take the Bishop: 18. Bxf7 + Kxf7 19. Qxh5 + Kg8 20. Rxg7 + !, and Black loses after 20 . . . Kxg7 21. Bxh6 + . Either Black then plays 21 . . . Kh7 or 21 . . . Kh8 or 21 . . . Kf6—all losing the Queen to 22. Bg5 + . Or Black retreats his King to g8 allowing Qg6 + and mate next on g7.
2) Black could move his King toward the center: 18. Bxf7 + Kf8, and Black is in mucho trouble after 19. Bxh6!.
3) Black could flee with his King to the corner: 18. Bxf7 + Kh8, when the simple 19. Bxh5 leaves White with a strong position.

CONCEPT: Don't play for traps riddled with drawbacks and that work only if your opponent blunders. Should he fail to blunder, you've merely worsened your position. Instead, set up soundly based traps that, regardless how your opponent responds, do not compromise your game.

Still, White is threatening the debilitating 18. Bxh6, capitalizing on the pinned g-pawn.

Black enters the maelstrom with **17 . . . Bg4!!.**

Q: Doesn't this lose a piece?

On the surface, the Bishop's protection can be erased with check, and afterward the Bishop can be safely captured. Thus 18. Nxf6 + Qxf6 19. Rxg4 seems to win the Bishop. This tactic is called *undermining* or "removing the defender" or "removing the guard." It aims to win an enemy unit by first removing its protection through capture or by chasing its protector away. The ensuing tactical melee in this particular case is complex and double-edged.

CONCEPT: Look for ways to undermine an enemy piece or pawn by capturing or driving away its support.

White removes the Bishop's guard with **18. Nxf6 + .**

Q: After the logical 18 . . . Qxf6, should White capture Black's Bishop with his Rook or Queen?

White must take the Bishop with his Rook, for 18 . . . Qxf6 19. Qxg4 falls for mate in one move by 19 . . . Re1—a back-rank checkmate. This is just one of the ways a Rook can deliver mate and is known as a *mating pattern,* referring to either the way mate is given or to how it appears visually. The more mating patterns you know, the more weapons you have in planning out your moves.

For example, if attacking with a Rook and Bishop, you might ask: What mates are possible with a Rook and Bishop? If you know the answer, then you naturally should ask the next question: Are any of those mates possible in my own situation? If the answer to this question is no, then you should ask the logical follow-up: Can I play in such a way that I maximize the chance for this mate to happen? And so on. This process of asking questions to determine plans and strategies is called the *analytic method.*

> SMYSLOV: Chess playing demands the development of ana-lytical skill. The ability to analyze is a very important quality for the improvement of a player, helping him to realize his errors and mistakes not only at the chessboard, but also, probably, in life.

CONCEPT: Study mating patterns and try to set them up in your own games. Develop a sensitivity for what is possible with different combinations of pieces and pawns.

Black takes back **18 . . . Qxf6.**

Q: Is 18 . . . gxf6 worth considering?

That would only justify White's play by exposing the King to terrible hazards. Not only would the g-file then be open, but Black's isolated h-pawn would be too frail to keep away the wolves, which include a Queen, a Rook, and two hungry Bishops.

White takes the Bishop, **19. Rxg4.**

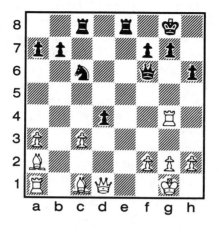

Q: *Who's ahead here, and by how much?*

Assuming Black takes White's pawn on c3, the difference will be that White will have two Bishops against a Knight and two pawns, giving White a slight material edge. In making these calculations, one goes through a process of counting and comparing—pawns against pawns, minor pieces against minor pieces, Rooks against Rooks, and Queen against Queen—noting the kinds of disparities as much as their actual values.

CONCEPT: Think of material differences in clear, exact terms. For example, don't say you're ahead by three points. Say you have an extra Bishop, or a Rook against two pawns, or a Queen against a Rook and pawn, and so on. This gives you more useful information and assists in forming an appropriate plan.

Black grabs a pawn with **19 . . . dxc3.**

Q: *How would you evaluate this position?*

Materially, White is a little ahead, having two Bishops for a Knight and two pawns. But Black does have counterplay. He's completely developed, with his Rooks aggressively positioned, especially the Rook at e8. Both his Knight and Queen also occupy useful pivot points.

Contrast this buildup with White's, who still hasn't moved his Queen-Rook or Bishop. If you don't use your extra piece, what good is it? White must be careful, in fact, not to get his King caught on the first rank. He may have to spend a tempo giving his King some breathing space. Black's real compensation is the passed c-pawn. This is ready to menace an advance and meantime guards key squares, restricting White's mobility. White must play from here very carefully.

White finally develops his dark-square Bishop **20. Be3.**

Q: *Why didn't White instead play 20. Rf4? Doesn't that skewer the Queen and f-pawn, winning the pawn?*

On 20. Rf4?, Black's surprise was 20 . . . c2, simultaneously attacking White's Queen and threatening mate. White's hanging Rook at a1 is gravy. Passed pawns can be quite dangerous. Use them unmercifully.

CONCEPT: Once you obtain a passed pawn, expedite its advance so that it distracts the enemy from his own plans and threatens to Queen. It's a maxim: Passed pawns must be pushed!

Black lunges forward with **20 . . . c2.**

Q: *What are the Black threats?*

In addition to the attacks to the Queen and Rook at a1 (if White takes the c-pawn with his Queen), Black has the centralization Ne5 followed by a subsequent Nd3, squaring away at the promotion square c1.

White's Queen escapes **21. Qf1?.**

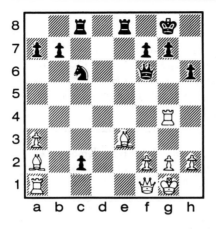

Q: *How does this move compare with 21. Qe1 instead?*

After 21. Qe1, Black extracts advantage with 21 . . . Rc-d8!, threatening 22 . . . Qxa1 followed by 23 . . . Rd1 +. So logic supports 22. Bb3, attacking the pawn and additionally guarding d1, preventing the sacrifice at a1 as in the previous note. And after 22. Bb3 (22. Rc1 Qb2 threatens the Bishop and menaces the Queen sacrifice on c1, followed by a Rook check on d1) 22 . . . Qb2 23. Ba4 b5, White must lose material. The move 21. Qf1, however, loses sooner.

Black tumbles the wall with **21 . . . Rxe3!!.**

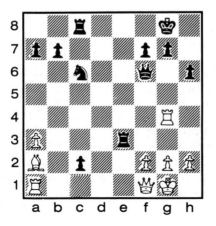

Q: What's the point?

Black is going to convert this confusing position into a winning endgame by simplifying and exploiting the indefensible weaknesses. To reach the endgame as soon as possible, he's even going to trade Queens. Then Black's dangerous c-pawn will prove decisive.

KASPAROV: Positions of this type demand clear-cut, specific action, with the aim of disclosing as quickly as possible the drawbacks of the opponent's setup.

CONCEPT: Exchange Queens if you want to facilitate the transition to the endgame.

White kills the Rook **22. fxe3.**

Q: Should Black interpolate 22 . . . Ne5, attacking the Rook before trading Queens?

This only delays matters and may actually equip White with defensive resources, such as 23. Rf4, preventing the Queen trade and piling up on f7.

CONCEPT: Don't vacillate. Once you've decided on a course of action, implement it directly. If you switch or delay plans, you may give your opponent time to save the game.

Black dissolves Queens with **22 . . . Qxf1 +.**

Q: What are the relative merits of taking back with the King instead of the Rook?

Taking back with the King brings it closer to the center, a basic endgame principle. But that leads to 23 . . . Ne5 threatening the Rook at g4 and the march of the c-pawn, backed up by the Rook. Note that Black is presently down a Rook and needs to act quickly before White can organize his forces. If he had the time, White would surely win with his extra material.

Taking back with the rook threatens Black's f-pawn, which may gain enough time to get his pieces working.

CONCEPT: When taking back, do so to gain time, to seize or maintain the initiative.

White sweeps up the Queen with **23. Rxf1.**

Q: How can Black combine an attack with defense?

By playing 23 . . . Ne5, Black's Knight defends f7 and gains time by hitting the Rook at g4.

CONCEPT: When defending, try to find moves that deal with the problem but coincidentally pose counterthreats. You may be able to steal the initiative and shred your opponent's attack.

Black centralizes the Knight with **23 . . . Ne5.**

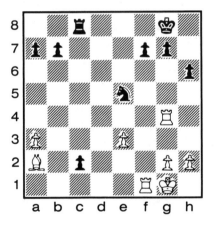

Q: Does 24. Bxf7 + save the day?

It may if Black answers it with 24 . . . Nxf7, when 25. Rc1 Ne5 26. Rd4 threatens 27. Rd2, winning the obstreperous c-pawn. Unfortunately for White, Black can respond to 24.

Bxf7 + by 24 . . . Kh8, keeping his Knight poised on e5 and
retaining threats to the Rook on g4 and the Rook on f1 (with
the advance of the c-pawn). Black's got the situation in hand.
A sample variation is 24. Bxf7 + Kh8 25. Rgf4 c1(Q) 26. Rxc1
Rxc1 + 27. Kf2 Nd3 + , garnering the exchange—A Knight for
a Rook.

White doubles up his Rooks **24. Rg-f4.** Black promotes **24
. . . c1(Q).**

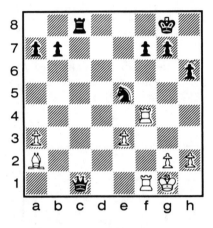

**Q: Does White have any solid chances to draw this end-
ing?**

Barring a chess miracle, White, down a pawn and about to
lose more, has little prospect of salvation. The hour of retribu-
tion—for attacking prematurely—is near.

White takes the Queen **25. Rxc1.**

Q: How might careless play endanger White's Bishop?

If White lets his guard down and answers 25 . . . Rxc1 +
with 26. Kf2, he would lose the Bishop to the forking check 26
. . . Rc2t. Another way Black could win after 26. Kf2 is 26 . . .
Nd3 + , forking King and Rook. It looks dismal for White.

Black gives check by **25 . . . Rxc1 + .**

Q: *What is White's only reasonable move?*

White must counter with his Rook if he is to avoid the horrendous variations in the previous note.

White blocks the check **26. Rf1.**

Q: *Without trading Rooks, how can Black now win a pawn?*

Black can fork the isolated a- and e-pawns by 26 . . . Rc3, which should ultimately lead to a win. But Black could win a pawn and also simplify further with another move.

Black eliminates the Rooks with **26 . . . Rxf1 + .**

Q: *Why is this trade a more exact method of winning than 26 . . . Rc3?*

Whereas 26 . . . Rc3 keeps the Rooks on the board, the trade reduces possible enemy counterplay. This sharpens Black's advantage.

CONCEPT: When ahead in material, trade pieces; when behind, avoid trades.

White takes back **27. Kxf1.**

Q: *Does White's Bishop give him sufficient hope for counterplay?*

Not at all. Black has a really good Knight anyway. More important is that Black has an extra pawn and is about to win more.

CONCEPT: Use your extra material to make more material: material makes material.

Black mops up with **27 . . . Ng4.**

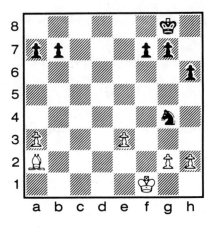

Q: Can White avoid the loss of a pawn?

No. Either he loses his e-pawn or h-pawn, leaving Black two pawns ahead, with an easily won endgame. Black would then have pawn majorities on both sides of the board. After centralizing his King, he would produce passed pawns in both sectors and force White's Bishop into early retirement.

White Resigns

POSTSCRIPT

This game was both typical and atypical of Yusupov's style. Normally he likes to build his games slowly out of the opening, pressing quietly for positional advantages. It's a controlled style and well suited to his ability to nurse microscopic nuances. But should the opponent confuse this surface tranquility for peaceableness, leading Yusupov into hand-to-hand combat, he will be ruefully surprised. For Yusupov, like most of his Russian colleagues, wields a devastating tactical sword that can be unsheathed at a moment's notice, as Pancyk learned to his dismay.

White made several mistakes this game. He neglected his development and then he proceeded to attack without sound positional justification. His initiative therefore proved to be transitory. With a few bold counterstrokes, Black broke White's attack for an offensive of his own. But unlike White, Black was positionally correct and his attack rolled merrily along to its logical conclusion. In the end, Black's Knight and five pawns would have proved too strong for White's Bishop and three pawns. This was a fine example of a great counterpuncher repulsing an unsound attack.

BOTVINNIK: A game of counterchances adequately cancels out the advantage of the first move. With such a method of playing the opening—ignoring symmetrical moves and aiming at counterplay—the advantage of the first move is less perceptive. This is in my view what present-day players aim at when playing Black.

Open Center, Queenside Castling, and Space

WHITE: Dolmatov
BLACK: Rogers
Tallin 1985

WHAT TO LOOK FOR

Black tries to swarm the center by storm, bringing his Queen to the front lines at once. White capitalizes on this premature development, exploiting the enemy Queen's misfortunes to gradually build up his own position so that his pieces enjoy superior mobility. Both players castle Queenside, which proves rather precarious for Black, who displaces pieces toward the Kingside for an unproductive attack. White winds up pressure-cooking Black on the Queenside with airtight compression tactics. Step by step, White's early initiative mounts to an all-powerful advantage that proves irresistible as Black succumbs.

THE CENTER COUNTER GAME

Of all the partially open games, this oldest one goes back more than 400 years. Its purpose is to create counteractivity for pieces in the center by an early development of Black's Queen. But Black's Queen sortie loses time, and without a real foothold in the center (no pawns), White wrests a permanent initiative throughout the game. Thus the Center Counter has found a home in the theoretical junkyards—until some genius revives it.

QUEENSIDE CASTLING

Commonly referred to as "castling long," Queenside castling entails a whole set of principles and themes not ordinarily found in games in the usual castling on the Kingside. Among the differences are the weakness to the a-pawn (lacking defense by the King) and the immediate positioning of a Rook on the d-file for attack. Often, as in this game, it is useful to shift the castled King to the b-file to lock the Queenside door, and you can develop remarkably quick attacks by shifting your Rook along the d-file to its 3rd or 4th rank for transfer elsewhere.

THE CENTRAL FILES

Much of the action takes place here. White has the only foothold in the center—the pawn at d4. He occupies e5 with a Knight to induce the weakening advance f6, which makes Black's e-pawn vulnerable along the e-file. Later, White maneuvers his Rook up to d3 and over to b3. White's greater control of the central lines eventually decides the game.

White commences 1. **e4.**

Q: *How does this move weaken f3?*

In the initial position, the square f3 is guarded no less than four times: directly by the pawns at e2 and g2 and the Knight at g1; indirectly by the Queen x-raying through the e-pawn. After 1. e4, White's strength on f3 is reduced. Should remaining defenders of f3 be removed, disaster can strike as in the following mini-game from a Russian novice tournament: 1. e4 Nc6 2. g3 Nd4 3. Ne2?? Nf3 mate. A more sophisticated version of the same trap is 1. e4 e5 2. Nf3 Nc6 3. Bc4 Nd4 4. Nxe5 Qg5 5. Nxf7 Qxg2 6. Rf1 Qxe4+ 7. Be2 Nf3 mate.

Naturally, the move 1. e4 cannot be censured on grounds that it weakens f3. The pluses—central control and open lines for development—far outweigh the potential weakening of f3, and in the fairytales given above, White could easily have averted the final catastrophes. What these examples illustrate is that every pawn move, regardless of its inherent strength, contains a weakness.

Black rough-houses with **1 . . . d5.**

Q: What move would Black like to see as a reply to 1 . . . d5?

Black yearns for White to play 2. e5. Though not a bad move in that it gains space, it reduces the central tension, enabling Black to pursue his own game freely with time to roundly complete his development. Play might proceed: 2 . . . Bf5 3. d4 e6 4. Nf3 c5 5. c3 Nc6, and Black has a comfortable game.

CONCEPT: If White wants to maintain the advantage of his inherent initiative from first-move superiority, he should look for ways to give his opponent problems.

White engages Black with **2. exd5.**

Q: Would it have been more prudent to protect the e-pawn by 2. Nc3?

Like the advance 2. e5, 2. Nc3 doesn't irk Black with serious problems. Black can choose between 2 . . . dxe4 3. Nxe4 e5 or 2 . . . d4 3. Nc-e2 e5, both of which leave him with excellent prospects. The merits of 2. exd5 are twofold. First, White temporarily obtains a pawn, though if Black plays correctly he will get it back. Second, the exchange knocks out Black's center pawn, allowing White to get a subsequent spatial advantage with the move d4.

CONCEPT: If you have a menaced pawn that can be salvaged by either protecting it, pushing it, or exchanging it for another pawn, you can most often gain time by exchanging. The other player generally has to waste a move to take it back, whereas the other two possibilities usually permit him to go on with his own game, frequently without having to respond to a definite threat.

Black takes the dive **2 . . . Qxd5.**

Q: *Instead of taking the pawn back immediately, could Black play 2 . . . Nf6?*

This alternative—known as the Marshall Variation—is a nice choice. The key question then is can White keep his extra pawn on d5? He can on the surface with 3. c4 (another try is 3. Bb5 + Bd7 4. Bc4), but Black can counter with a promising gambit: 3 . . . c6 4. dxc6 Nxc6, followed by 5 . . . e5. In the resulting positions, White's additional pawn is balanced for Black by the ease with which his remaining forces can be developed and by his expansive spatial advantage. In this line White's d-pawn plays a purely defensive role at d3, restricting the scope of his light-square Bishop. And the d-pawn may become weak if Black posts a Bishop at f5 and Rooks along the d-file.

White therefore usually foregoes trying to hold the pawn, letting it hang by playing 3. d4. This at least stakes White's claim in the center and augments his space. And if Black plays the anticipated 3 . . . Nxd5, White can shoo away the Knight with the advance c4.

CONCEPT: Don't compromise your position irrelevantly by gobbling up "poisoned pawns," especially in the opening when time is crucial.

White assails the Queen with **3. Nc3.**

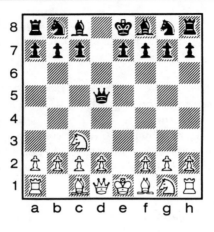

Q: *Does this move gain White anything?*

White surely gains time by attacking Black's Queen, forcing it to move. Many writers state matter-of-factly that 3. Nc3 actually refutes Black's opening. Ah, if chess were only that simple! In reality, by playing 2 . . . Qxd5, Black gains a developing tempo in effect, so White's 3. Nc3 merely redresses the equilibrium.

A more fundamental question is: Which piece—Black's Queen or White's Knight—is more effectively developed? Masters and theoreticians alike concur that White's Knight has found its most suitable square at c3, while Black's Queen must still search. But who can tell so early the most efficacious place for the Queen? Her only choice now is to move again—probably not to the best square either.

CONCEPT: Don't commit too much power early in the game. You may suddenly need it elsewhere and would be powerless to turn it on. Hold back the Queen and Rooks in the opening stages until it's clearly evident how they can best be employed.

Black gets out of the oven **3 . . . Qa5.**

Q: *Would it have been sagacious to retreat the Queen to d8 instead?*

After 3 . . . Qd8 4. d4, it's clear that White's third move truly has gained a full tempo, as Black's Queen in effect hasn't moved, now back on its original square. If tempi were the only factor, then 3 . . . Qa5 is superior to 3 . . . Qd8. But there are other considerations, such as safety. At d8, the Queen is far safer than at a5, where it soon faces attack. And from d8 Black's Queen guards more of the center, especially d5 and d4. But mentors disagree on which move is really better, so it's rather a matter of choice. If 3 . . . Qa5 disturbs you, then 3 . . . Qd8 is an acceptable alternative.

White strikes at the midsection with **4. d4.**

Q: Is this White's best?

Years of chess practice confirm that it is, but concrete verification cannot be provided. The best way to learn is to work it out by yourself. Analytically, White does about as well with 4. Nf3 and 4. Bc4—often transposing to the same lines anyway. But **4. d4** makes the most practical sense because this move must be played eventually if White is to extract advantage. Since there's no tactical disadvantage inherent in **4. d4,** why not play it at once?

CONCEPT: Rely finally on your own powers. Don't mechanically follow the opinion of so-called authorities. Even if you go astray in making your own decisions and judgments, you may learn from your mistakes and thereby discern the real basis for choosing the other moves.

> **BOTVINNIK: Chess, like any creative activity, can exist only through the combined efforts of those who have creative talent, and those who have the ability to organize their creative work.**

CONCEPT: When you must choose between several reasonable moves, pick the one that gives you the most options. Play flexibly.

SPASSKY: I try as a rule to play evenly, and carefully take the measure of my dangerous opponents.

Black perks up with **4 . . . Nf6.**

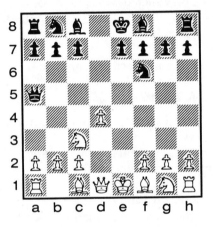

Q: *How flexible is this move?*

Very pliable. In playing **4 . . . Nf6,** Black astutely develops and gives away few of his intentions. This is the best square for the King-Knight in most variations. Less adaptable would be:

A) 4 . . . Nc6, which would be answered by 5. Bb5 or the chasing 5. d5.

B) 4 . . . Nd7, which is less aggressive and temporarily obstructs the light-square Bishop.

C) 4 . . . e6, which hems in the light-square Bishop more permanently.

D) 4 . . . Bf5, which is fair, though it cedes the opportunity to answer 5. Nf3 with 5 . . . Bg4 without wasting a tempo.

E) 4 . . . e5, called Anderssen's Variation, which is very risky. It was popular in the mid-nineteenth century and has fallen into disuse. The reason is was jettisoned is that, being behind in development, it behooves Black to avoid opening the center. White is simply better able to take advantage of it.

CONCEPT: Don't open lines unless you are better developed. You may be digging your own grave.

ALEKHINE: Don't open fresh lines to a better-developed opponent.

White erects his game with **5. Nf3.**

Q: To avoid being pinned, should White have first played 5. h3?

Before you answer this question you may want to examine the variation continuing **5. Nf3** Bg4 6. Bc4. After 6. Bc4 Black plays 6 . . . Nc6 with the better of it. He threatens White's d-pawn and plans to intensify the pressure by castling Queenside and advancing e5, attacking the potentially pinned d-pawn. White indeed should be concerned with this pin.

The drawback to 5. h3, however, is that it doesn't develop anything. Yes, it aids White's game, but it doesn't bring out a new piece to build his position. Still, it turns out that White can play this move to advantage, not on the 5th move but on the 6th. After **5. Nf3** Bg4, then White can play 6. h3. If Black follows with 6 . . . Bxf3 7. Qxf3 Nc6, White has the powerful rejoinder 8. Bb5!, his own private pin. In this line 6. h3 loses no move because it compels Black's Bishop to make tracks for a second time.

Black plays the anticipated **5 . . . Bg4.**

Q: Should Black instead attack the pinned Knight at c3 by 5 . . . Ne4?

That move is a lemon. White surehandedly plays 6. Bd2, and regardless whether Black trades on d2 or c3, he loses time and builds White's game. If White is frisky, he can even gambit a pawn for development with 6. Bd3 Nxc3 7. bxc3 Qxc3+ 8. Bd2. In exchange for the pawn, White has three tempi: three pieces out to Black's one, and he will have the chance to develop a fourth piece after Black rescues his Queen. A rule of thumb is that, in the opening, three developed pieces are worth a pawn.

A handy method for counting tempi in this opening is to see how many moves are required to connect the Rooks:

White can connect his Rooks after:

1) Castling (0-0).
2) Moving his Queen (Qe2).

Black can connect his Rooks after:

1) Developing his Knight at b8.
2) A pawn move (e6 or g6).
3) A move for the dark-square Bishop.
4) A move for the light-square Bishop.
5) Castling (0-0 or 0-0-0).

Black thus needs five moves to White's two to connect the Rooks, which means that White is ahead by three tempi. He would have enough compensation for his gambited pawn.

CONCEPT: In many situations, you can determine who has a lead in development by comparing how long it takes for each side to connect his Rooks. The sooner you can connect, the more developed you are.

White plays out his hand **6. h3.**

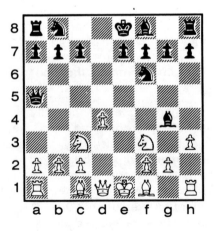

Q: *How does White answer Black's 6 . . . Qh5?*

White, of course, should avoid the breakup of his Kingside pawns ensuing from the pending exchange on f3. He has a solid position-building move, however, in 7. Be2. If Black then continues with 7 . . . Bxf3, White has a powerful game after taking back on f3 with his Bishop. Probably Black would speculate with 7 . . . e6, so that after 8. 0-0, he can poise an attack on White's King. Two risky lines are 8 . . . Bd6 9. hxg4 Nxg4, and 8 . . . Bxh3 9. gxh3 Qxh3.

In either case, Black gets too little compensation for his sacrificed material. White's central space and stellar development insure his means to repel Black's cutthroat tactics. Still, White would have to play very carefully to realize his advantage. One false step could prove fatal, given his King's exposed position.

CONCEPT: Bluff your opponent, as in poker. Look for ways to entice him into unsound sacrifices. Then play accurately and convert your material gain into victory.

> **PETROSIAN:** I had the fixed idea of luring my opponent forward, giving him the possibility of attack, in order—if the attack did not lead to success—of leaving him no better off than when he began.

Black steps back **6 . . . Bh5.**

Q: *How does the trade 6 . . . Bxf3 lose time?*

After 7. Qxf3, the threat to take on b7 leaves Black no time to redress the balance of the developing tempi. The move 7 . . . Nc6 would do it, but unfortunately for Black, it's unplayable, for the pinning 8. Bb5 is too strong. Black probably has to guard b7 by playing 7 . . . c6, which hardly develops anything. Using our method of counting tempi, White needs three moves to connect his Rooks, while Black needs four. This represents a net gain for White of one tempo, which adds to his initial advantage of having the first move. Thus Black loses a move because of 6 . . . Bxf3.

White wisely breaks the pin on his c3-Knight with **7. Bd2.**

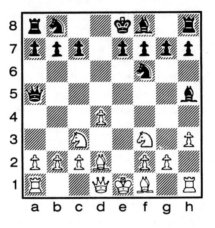

SPASSKY: This is perhaps not the best move in the position, but it's part of a definite plan and that's good.

Q: How does White now meet 7 . . . Nc6?

As in prior variations, the correct response is 8. Bb5, pinning the Knight. At b5, the Bishop also threatens sometime to splinterize Black's Queenside with a subsequent Bxc6. For example, if Black castles Queenside (8 . . . 0-0-0), White jounces with 9. Bxc6 bxc6 10. g4 Bg6 11. Ne5, threatening 12. Nxc6, winning a Rook for a Knight.

After 7 . . . Nc6 8. Bb5, Black could try 8 . . . Qb6 to avoid doubled c-pawns, but that runs into a nasty trap: 9. g4 Bg6 10. g5. And if the Knight moves, say 10 . . . Nd7, White wins the Queen with 11. Nd5, for 11 . . . Qxb5 Nxc7+ crunches.

Another question is why does Dolmatov avoid playing the main line: that is, instead of **7. Bd2,** why doesn't he play 7. g4

Bg6 8. Ne5—the recommended continuation in opening manuals? I don't know—it may have something to do with psychology. It's speculated that Dolmatov, a student of the world's most cunning chess trainer, Mark Dvoretsky, is reflecting his opponent's knowledge of the opening. Ian Rogers, an Australian grandmaster, is a leading authority on the Center Counter Defense. Both Dvoretsky and Dolmatov know it's best to get one's opponent out of the familiar into the uncomfortable as soon as possible. It can be suicide to fight a man on his own turf. Nonetheless, Dolmatov must feel that **7. Bd2** is also a good move, else he wouldn't play it no matter what.

POLUGAEVSKY: An ancient chess truth: First and foremost it is essential to understand the essence, the overall idea of any fashionable variation, and only then include it in one's opening repertoire. Otherwise the tactical tries will conceal from the player the strategic picture of the board, in which his orientation will most likely be lost.

CONCEPT: For psychological and practical reasons, don't play into an opponent's knowledge. Get him "out of his books" as soon as you can. It deprives him of his greatest weapon—his knowledge—and may make him uneasy.

Black clears a diagonal with **7 . . . e6.**

Q: *What two pawns did White tactically weaken by 7. Bd2?*

By playing **7. Bd2** White leaves his b-pawn unprotected and cuts the communication between his Queen and d-pawn. Black could simultaneously attack both of these pawns after 7 . . . Bxf3 8. Qxf3 Qb6, but not to his advantage. White simply castles Queenside, guarding the b-pawn with his King and dissuading Black from playing 9 . . . Qxd4 because of 10. Qxb7—a powerful invasion by White's Queen.

White debuts his King-Bishop **8. Bc4.**

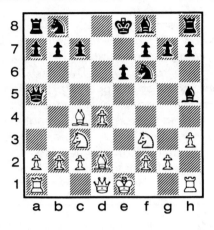

Q: *What does White now threaten?*

Merely to win Black's Queen. If Black plays routinely and overlooks the threat, say by 8 . . . Be7, then 9. Nd5 sweeps in Her Majesty. Since the only safe square for the Queen is a4, play should then proceed 9 . . . Qa4 10. Bb5 + ! Qxb5 11. Nxc7 + , forking King and Queen. This is the same problem as bringing out the Queen early: It's subject to persistent harassment and deadly traps. In this variation, and several others, notice how it's the minor pieces and pawns that pester the Queen most.

CONCEPT: In trying to exploit a prematurely exposed Queen, try to attack it with pawns and minor pieces, developing each one at the enemy Queen's expense.

Black finds a loophole with **8 . . . c6.**

Q: *How does this meet the threat?*

It opens the a5-d8 diagonal, giving Black's Queen a safe retreat. Thus, 9. Nd5 is answered by 9 . . . Qd8. This variation has been seen in several of Rogers's games, but Dolmatov knows this and is prepared to snag him with a different, though quite satisfactory move.

White slyly essays **9. Qe2.**

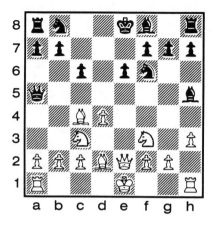

Q: Can Black now try 9 . . . Bxf3 10. Qxf3 Qb6?

This position is somewhat similar to one we looked at
before. Two aspects of it are different and favor Black: his
pawn at c6 blocks the attack along the f3-b7 diagonal, and
after taking the d-pawn with his Queen Black menaces the
Bishop at c4, gaining time. Even so, White has excellent
chances, represented by three sample lines following from the
moves 9 . . . Bxf3 10. Qxf3 Qb6 11. 0-0-0 Qxd4:

A) 12. Bg5 Qxc4 13. Bxf6 gxf6 14. Qxf6, threatening the Rook at
h8 and mate at d8.

B) 12. Bg5 Qe5 13. Ne4 Qxe4 14. Qxe4 Nxe4 15. Rd8 mate.
Once again, the d-file paves the way to White's victory.

C) 12. Bg5 Qe5 13. Ne4 Nb-d7 14. Rh-e1 Nxe4 15. Bf4 Qf5 16.
Rxe4 0-0-0. Here, it might seem that by castling, Black has
gotten through the worst, but after 17. Rxe6 fxe6 18. Qxc6 +
bxc6 19. Ba6 mate, the yoke's on him.

Naturally, these variations do not begin to exhaust the
position's immense possibilities, but they do show its vitality.
They also depict the risk one takes in moving his Queen too
many times in the opening.

> **GREKOV:** The Germanic player (Tarrasch, Maroczy, Schlechter) tends to ask: How is this position like every other position? The Russian tends to ask: How is this position different from every other position?

Black shields his Queen with **9 . . . Bb4.**

Q: Could 9 . . . Qf5 have been played?

Not safely. The crux is the variation 10. g4 Nxg4 11. Bd3! Qf6 12. hxg4 Bxg4 13. Be4, allowing White to keep his extra piece. Note the in-between move 11. Bd3!, before taking Black's Knight, gains time and enables the Bishop's repositioning to e4 to guard f3.

White breaks the pin with **10. g4.**

Q: What does this move suggest about the placement of White's King?

White plans to castle Queenside. If he had any intention of castling Kingside, he would have kept his pawn back on g2, where it along with the f- and h-pawns would form a defensive cocoon around a castled King.

Black saves his Bishop **10 . . . Bg6.**

Q: This Bishop has made three moves so far. Is that bad?

The rule is to move each piece just once in an opening, finding the best square for it and moving it there. Taking several moves for each piece wastes time and results in backward development.

This Bishop's case is not so clear, however, for its last two moves were made in response to White's pawn attacks, which cannot be considered true-developing moves.

While White's pawns have picked up some space on the Kingside with their forward movement, they've also caused some weaknesses—most notably, f4 and h4. Thus, the judgment on this Bishop so far is neutral. It now sits on a good square. Much will depend on how we ultimately evaluate White's Kingside pawns. Are they strong or weak?

POLUGAEVSKY: The boundless and inexhaustive nature of chess is in no way associated with the astronomical number of moves present in every position. The depth of chess lies in the wide variety of ideas and methods by which any position on the board is characterized, and in the exceptions which are almost always present in any particular piece arrangement.

White castles Queenside **11. 0-0-0.**

Q: Is it risky to castle Queenside?

Not really. White has enough defenders in the area to neutralize Black's aggressors. White moreover connects his Rooks, a main objective in the opening.

Black develops his Queen-Knight **11 . . . Nb-d7.**

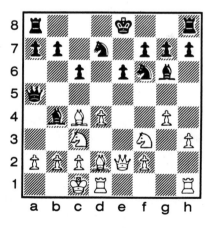

A big negative on that. If we had doubts about White's potentially weak Kingside pawns, this would dispel them. Here their advanced state would be put to effective use. In positions of opposite-side castling, each player tries to move the pawns on files in front of the enemy King to open pathways to it. It becomes a race, the winner being the player whose pawns get there first. The marching pawns can be used to breach the defensive pawn wall around the other side's King. After 11 . . . 0-0, clearly it's White who has a big head start in his pawn race. No, Black shouldn't castle Kingside.

POLUGAEVSKY: When play on the flanks begins, everything depends on who is the quicker.

CONCEPT: If castled on opposite sides, try to move the pawns on the files in front of your opponent's King.

CONCEPT: To develop your tactical skills, purposely castle on the opposite side from your opponent's King in practice games. Persistent exercises like this will hone your ingenuity in attack.

White closes shop with **12. Kb1.**

Q: Why does White play this?

It's a good housekeeping move. If castled on the Queenside, you have a broader front to guard. The King, in fact, does not protect the a-pawn. So it's fairly typical to move the King to b1 (or to b8) to assuage any potential weakness to the Rook-pawn. In this particular position, Kb1 has specific import. Suppose, for example, that instead of **12. Kb1** White plays 12. a3, attacking the Bishop. Black is under no real compulsion to move the Bishop and can continue 12 . . . Nb6. If White takes the Bishop, 13. axb4, then 13 . . . Qa1+ 14. Nb1 Na4 15. Bc3 Ne4 gives Black dangerous attack rumblings. A final point to 12. Kb1 is that it clears c1 for a piece, usually a Rook.

Black castles Queenside **12 . . . 0-0-0.**

Q: How would you assess the position?

Both sides have completed their development and connected their Rooks. White has the advantage in the center because of his pawn at d4, which gives him more space. All of White's pieces are on good squares, safe from attack. Two of Black's counterparts, the Queen and dark-square Bishop, can both be menaced by a possible advance a3. Overall, at the transition to the middlegame, White has some advantage in position. White's task is to make this advantage grow.

White attacks the Bishop with **13. a3.**

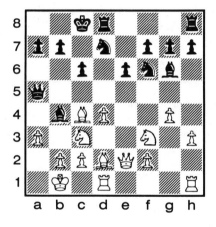

Q: Should White worry about the sacrifice 13 . . . Bxa3?

He doesn't have to. The move 13 . . . Bxa3 is truly an unsound sacrifice. After 13 . . . Bxa3 14. bxa3 Qxa3, White can safeguard his King by 15. Na2, followed by 16. Bb4 or 16. Bc1. In fact, after 13 . . . Bxa3, White even has 14. Nd5!, when 14 . . . Qa4 15. b3 wins the Queen. The whole idea recalls our discussion of 8 . . . Bxh3 in the question to **6. h3.** You mustn't throw your men away without a definite and clear purpose.

CONCEPT: Do not sacrifice without clear and verifiable reasons. If you can't justify a sacrifice concretely, you probably shouldn't make it.

CONCEPT: Often the best way to refute a sacrifice is to accept the offered material. You must put the burden on your opponent and make him prove that he really has compensation.

Black takes the Knight **13 . . . Bxc3.**

Q: Is this exchange good for Black?

It's the best of a bad bargain. Our analysis so far has ruled out 13 . . . Bxa3, and 13 . . . Bd6 loses material to 14. Nb5. The move 13 . . . Be7 also drops a piece to 14. Nd5 (note the discovery to Black's Queen), which leaves f8 as the only safe retreat square.

> **ALEKHINE:** The retreat of a minor piece to the back rank, where it cuts the lines of communication between the Rooks, is permissible only in exceptional cases.

In fact, after 13 . . . Bf8, White doesn't have anything dramatic, but he can improve his position with 14. Rh-e1, after which Black is hard pressed for an intelligent move. Ergo, there really is just one plausible move: **13 . . . Bxc3.** At least this reduces the pressure against Black's cramped position.

> **PETROSIAN:** The fewer pieces on the board, the fewer the number of squares you require to move about in.

The rub here is that of all Black's pieces, the one he might need the most is the dark-square Bishop. It guards some important squares. Just note the Black pawn structure. Five of his seven pawns occupy light squares, which creates gaps on the dark-squares. With the removal of this valiant defender, Black's game takes a turn for the worse.

CONCEPT: If your opponent is weak on squares of a particular color, try to exchange off the Bishop that guards the weakened squares.

White snaps back **14. Bxc3.**

Q: Is White's Bishop well placed at c3?

Not especially. It comes to this square in order to avoid busting up White's Queenside pawn structure. At c3, the Bishop's mobility is blocked by White's pawn at d4. If White could exchange this pawn for either Black's c- or e-pawns, the Bishop would suddenly come to life. After such an exchange, the Bishop would emerge as a tower of strength.

Black finds a cave to hide in **14 . . . Qc7.**

Q: Is this the best square for Black's Queen?

None of the other squares compare. The other two possibilities, Qb6 and Qa4, leave the Queen less centralized. And every other place is guarded by enemy forces.

White repositions his Bishop by **15. Bd2.**

Q: Should White instead have tried 15. Ne5?

Though not really a bad move, the centralization 15. Ne5 actually helps Black. The exchange 15 . . . Nxe5 16. dxe5 somewhat eases the cramp on Black's position and permits Black's f6-Knight to occupy the d5 square.

Black snakes in with **15 . . . Ne4.**

Q: Why does Black play this?

Black wants to exchange pieces, relieving the pressure on his game. In particular, he'd like to eliminate the dark-square

Bishop before it assumes a more commanding post. The problem with **15 . . . Ne4** is that the exchange can be avoided and the Knight can later be driven from this center square.

White insures his Bishop with **16. Bc1.**

Q: How does this retreat compare with the possibility of 13 . . . Bf8?

Both moves retreat a Bishop to the back rank, but Black's interferes with the commerce between the two Rooks along the first rank. No such objection can be lodged against the Bishop at c1, for the Queen-Rook is already developed. Of course, c1 is not the best post for the Bishop, but a straight-line piece like the Bishop can afford to lean back and wait for a suitable moment to engage the fray.

Black attacks a Bishop **16 . . . Nb6.**

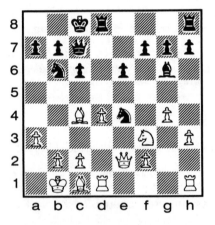

Q: Does Black mean to trade his Knight for White's Bishop?

No question about it. Again, the fewer pieces he has to move, the easier his defensive task. Failing this exchange, he'd like to position his Knight at d5.

White retreats the other Bishop **17. Bd3.**

Q: *Is it better to play 17. Bb3, and on 17 . . . Nd5, take the Knight?*

No, the Bishop would not be as useful at b3. First, White does not plan to trade his light-square Bishop for a Black Knight. A better plan is to preserve the Bishop and drive away a Knight on d5 by the push c4. To move the c-pawn safely, White must neutralize the Bishop at g6, which is one purpose of **17. Bd3.** The other reason is to dispel the ambitious Knight at e4.

Black pusillanimously drops back **17 . . . Nd6.**

Q: *What forceful move does this prevent White from playing?*

The retreat to d6 stops 18. c4, which would lose a pawn to either Knight. White couldn't defend himself because his Bishop at d3 would be pinned. Note that 17 . . . Nf6 fails to 18. c4, because 18 . . . Nxc4 19. Bxg6 hxg6 20. Qxc4 wins a Knight.

White centralizes his equus with **18. Ne5.**

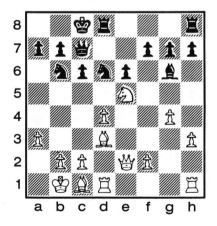

Q: *In chess terminology, is e5 an outpost or a hole?*

An *outpost* has a specific meaning. It is a square in the enemy camp, supported along a half-open or open file by a Rook or Queen and guarded also by a pawn, that can be occupied by a piece, particularly a Knight. The enemy may be able to control the outpost with a pawn. A *hole* designates a similar place, but one that is not vulnerable to pawn attack. With Black's pawn at f7 in our game, e5 is an outpost. If the pawn were at f5, however, e5 would be a hole.

Black trades Bishops **18 . . . Bxd3.**

Q: *Did Black make this trade because he feared an exchange on g6?*

Black does not object to such an exchange. Should it occur, Black would take back toward the center, opening the h-file. Black has a more subtle reason for trading Bishops. He has a Kingside majority of pawns that he'd like to set in motion. As long as the Bishop remains where it is, Black dare not move either his f-pawn or h-pawn for fear of losing a pawn on g6 after the Bishop is captured.

CONCEPT: If you have a pawn majority, use it. Don't disrupt it by exchanges.

White captures with his Rook **19. Rxd3.**

Q: *How do you evaluate White's alternative captures on d3?*

A) 19. cxd3 is dreadful. Apart from making it impossible to ever control d5 with a pawn this game, White drops the d-pawn to 19 . . . Nb5.
B) 19. Nxd3 is not bad, but the Knight is so much better placed at e5, it's shameful to remove it from that post.
C) 19. Qxd3 is an overuse of the Queen. Utilize the other pieces if they are to be effective. The White Queen is fine on e2, and from d3 it actually might become bothered by the Rook at d8.

D) 19. Rxd3 makes the most sense. It clears d1 for the other Rook and prepares to transfer this Rook where needed.

Black counterattacks with **19 . . . h5.**

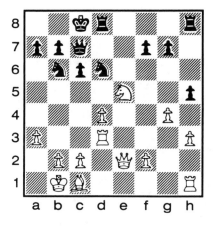

Q: What's behind this move?

To open the h-file for counterplay and to weaken White's g4. Some chessmasters actually feel strongly about the move h5, whatever circumstances it occurs under.

> **BRONSTEIN:** My favorite move [h5], with my favorite pawn, on my favorite square.

White doubles his Rooks **20. Rh-d1.**

Q: What do you think of 20. g5?

The advance 20. g5 is weak, for it creates a hole at f5 for Black to place a Knight. The same argument holds for the pawn impairing 20. gxh5, which also cedes f5. Note that a Black Knight placed at f5 hits White's d-pawn in conjunction with a Rook from d8.

CONCEPT: Try to create *batteries*, two pieces of like power aligned on the same rank, file, or diagonal. Line up a Queen and Bishop, or a Queen and Rook, or two Rooks. Doubled pieces amount to greater strength.

Black takes a pawn **20 . . . hxg4.**

Q: Wouldn't it be better for Black to delay exchanging, retaining the right to play a subsequent h4?

No. The advance h4 isn't even in the cards and offers Black nothing. Much better to open the h-file for use by the Rook, and much more consistent.

White retakes **21. hxg4.**

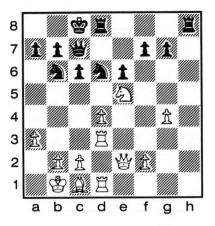

Q: Why not instead 21. Qxg4, attacking Black's g-pawn?

Forget about 21. Qxg4—it abandons f5 to Black's d6 Knight. Dolmatov's strategy consists of restricting the black Knights by careful placement of his own pawns. Right now the White pawn at g4 hems in the Knight beautifully, and White shouldn't release the pressure by a careless exchange.

CONCEPT: The best way to restrict the enemy pieces is by a judicious placement of your own pawns. The enemy pieces simply cannot land safely on squares the pawns control.

Black inches up with **21 . . . Rh7.**

**Q: *Should Black instead aim toward trading Knights by 21
. . . Nb-c4?***

In principle it seems plausible. The problem is it doesn't work tactically. If 21 . . . Nb-c4, then 22. b3. If Black completes the transaction, 22 . . . Nxe5, then 23. dxe5 and Black's remaining Knight faces some music. For example, 23 . . . Ne8 breaks the Rook communication and loses to 24. Rxd8 +. On the other hand, 23 . . . Nb5 allows White to trap the Knight by 23. a4.

White guards more territory with **22. b3.**

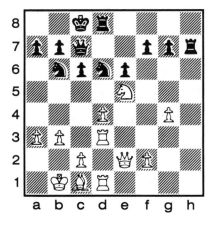

**Q: *Does this weaken the pawn skeleton around White's
King?***

It does breach White's Queenside security, but is nevertheless valid. If you play with a blind trumpeting of rules of thumb, you might never consider powerful iconoclastic moves such as **22. b3.** A great strength of the younger Russian school is their ability to size up a position concretely, to discover those features that constitute a law unto itself. They do not break many practical guidelines so much as uncover new ones. They see chess as Discovery Land. The old rules have merit, but the young Russians see the road to chess mastery as marked by question marks along the way that challenge tradition.

Dolmatov (White) here has weighed the benefits of **22. b3.** In exchange for the capacity to mobilize his Queenside pawns, he weakens his King's position. He reasons, however, that Black is in no position to exploit his weakened King's position. If a weak pawn cannot be attacked, in essence it's not really weak.

CONCEPT: Use rules, principles, theoretical suggestions, and the like as guidelines, not as absolute dicta. Understand when they apply and when they don't. Judge every position concretely on its own merits. There is no substitute for analysis—no smooth royal road to the royal game.

CONCEPT: Question every concept you've read in this or any other book if it doesn't seem right in a particular instance. Make sure you understand how each is applicable, as well as all its limitations.

Black drives out the Knight **22 . . . f6.**

Q: Doesn't this move show that White's Knight excursion to e5 was a waste of time?

No. the occupation of a Knight outpost shouldn't be viewed merely as an isolated sortie behind enemy lines. It was executed so that White could exploit his semi-open e-file. In this context, the Knight has performed yeomanlike work, for after its withdrawal from e5, Black's e6 square will be exposed to attack along the e-file. Black will become restricted in trying to uphold it.

CONCEPT: After your Knight has been driven from its outpost by a structure-softening pawn move, focus your attention on the weak enemy pawn in front of the square the Knight occupied. Confront it along the half-open file you occupy and from elsewhere. Its defense could drain blood from your opponent's entire game.

White withdraws the Knight **23. Nf3.**

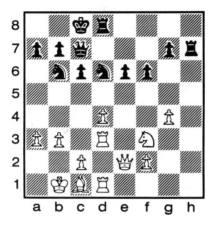

Q: Wouldn't plunging into Black's backyard by 23. Ng6 be more potent?

It would be an erroneous invasion. Two indicative variations are:

- A) 23. Ng6 Qf7 24. Nf4 Re8 25. Re3 Nd5! (forcing White to agree to an exchange of Knights) 26. Nxd5 exd6, and Black's worries are behind him.
- B) 23. Ng6 Qf7 24. Nf4 Re8 25. Re1 Nd5! 26. Nxe6 Nb5! 27. Kb2 Nb-c7, and suddenly it's clear that in capturing on e6 White's Knight has stepped into the lion's den.

Dolmatov's simple retreat avoids all these potential pitfalls and gives White a solid initiative against the e-pawn, probably drawing Black's Queen over to defend it away from the Queenside.

Black strengthens his e-pawn with **23 . . . Qf7.**

Q: Wouldn't it be better to leave the Queen on the Queen-side and defend by 23 . . . Re8?

There's no pat answer to this one, for each Black defense has frailties. One reason to move the Queen off c7 is to avoid dangerous pinning possibilities, following from Bf4, c4 and c5, which would win Black's Knight at d6. From f7, the Queen also has the possibility of becoming active at g6. Probably, Qf7 has slightly more going for it than Re8.

White expands with **24. c4.**

Q: What's White's threat?

White plans the fork of Knights by 25. c5. One of the two Knights therefore should now move.

Black sidesteps the danger with **24 . . . Nd7.**

Q: Would sacrificing a Knight at c4 be viable?

After 24 . . . Nbxc4 25. bxc4 Nxc4, Black obtains two pawns for his Knight plus permanent use of the d5 square. But the Knight has no comrades to support its attack, so there's really no danger posed to White's King. It surely relieves some of Black's problems temporarily, but in the long run most lose to precise defense—the kind Dolmatov can easily muster.

PETROSIAN: Turning chess into poker and hoping for a bluff is not one of my convictions.

White regroups with **25. Qe1.**

Q: Is this a pointless retreat?

Not at all. Since the 9th move White's Queen has been waiting patiently on e2 to toe into the fracas. Sixteen moves later, the position has assumed a definite shape and Dolmatov knows where he wants to commit his most powerful piece. He wants to play it to a5, to exploit the weakened dark squares in the vicinity of Black's King, which is a cog in a general campaign on the Queenside.

CONCEPT: Budget your thinking. Look for general plans and strategies when it's your opponent's turn, when your mind can wander more freely. On your own turn, get specific and determine the best move.

Black maneuvers his Knight with **25 . . . Nf8.**

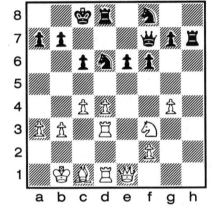

Q: Why this fallback?

Black needs to release his Queen from the e-pawn's protection, enabling her to attack from g6 or defend from c7.

White seeks a place in the sun with **26. Kb2.**

Q: Why not 26. Qa5 immediately?

The Queen's move 26. Qa5 would be premature, and Black could actually ignore for now the attack to his a-pawn. After 26. Qa5 Qg6! 27. Qxa7, Black has the startling 27 . . . Rh1!, disrupting White's harmony. Note that 28. Rxh1 then loses a piece to 28 . . . Qxd3 + followed by 29 . . . Qxf3. By playing

26. Kb2, White averts any future pinning surprises along the b1-h7 diagonal.

Black ups the ante with **26 . . . g5.**

Q: Why does Black play this?

For several reasons:

1) To prevent White's Bishop from occupying f4.
2) To prepare a Knight's maneuver to f4 (f8-g6-f4).
3) To clear his 2nd rank so that Black's Rook at h7 can shift to the Queenside for defense.

White pushes ahead with **27. a4.**

Q: Why this advance?

It steals some space on the Queenside while depriving Black's Knight use of b5. White's attack is still in preparation and he wants to gather as many little advantages as he can before launching the final assault.

CONCEPT: Accumulate small advantages. Taken as a whole, they can amount to an overwhelming superiority that favorably upsets the dynamic equilibrium.

Black withdraws the Rook **27 . . . Rh8?.**

Q: How does this jibe with Black's previous move, 26 . . . g5?

To guard his Queenside, Black would like to shift his King to b8. If White's Queen plays to a5, however, it would be attacking Black's Rook at d8. By playing his other Rook back to the first rank, Black plans to move his Knight at f8 to reestablish communication between the Rooks on the back rank. But does he have time for all this?

White builds with **28. Be3.**

Q: How does White intend to meet 28 . . . Kb8?

Now that White has placed his Bishop on e3, his preparations are complete. He's ready for the breakthrough advance d5. Since Black will want to keep the center closed because he's not as well developed, he will answer 29. d5 with 29 . . . cxd5 30. cxd5 e5. White then smashes through, however, by 31. Bxa7 + ! Kxa7 32. Qa5 +, picking up the Rook at d8. The fuse has been lit. The game is about to explode.

Black safeguards with **28 . . . a6.**

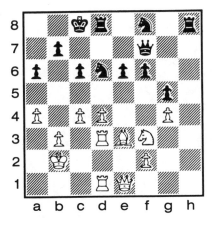

Q: What about blocking the Bishop's line with 28 . . . b6 instead of 28 . . . a6?

It offers both merits and demerits. After 28 . . . b6 29. d5, Black blunts the attack by 29 . . . exd5 30. cxd5 c5. Unfortunately for Black, White's game is so strong that he can blithely switch plans. Exploiting the fresh weakness at b6, White could continue 29. c5!, which leads to the opening of the c-file. Neither pawn advance ultimately saves the game.

White zooms in with **29. d5!.**

Q: What does White threaten?

The impending blow is 30. dxc6 bxc6 31. Rxd6, winning a Knight. White's attack now proceeds with fervor.

Black takes **29 . . . cxd5.**

Q: Would 29 . . . exd5 be better?

Not really. After 29 . . . exd5 30. cxd5, the only way Black can keep the d-file closed is to surrender a pawn for nothing by 30 . . . c5 31. Bxc5. This would only delay Black's capitulation for a few moves.

White recaptures **30. cxd5.**

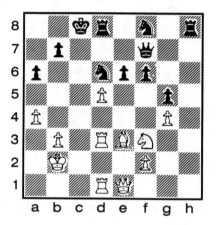

Q: How significant is the opening of the c-file for White's Rooks?

After Black plays 30 . . . e5, the c-file would be the only usable channel to the Black position. In order to conduct the attack, White needs open routes into the heart of the enemy camp. Any of the three vertical rows on the Queenside (the a-, b-, or c-files) would suffice, depending on which actually becomes clear. Black, since he can't keep all these lines closed, must decide which one will hurt him the least.

Black keeps the d-file closed with **30 . . . e5.**

Q: Should Black have braved it out with 30 . . . exd5?

After 30 . . . exd5 31. Rxd5, Black cannot match White on the d-file as illustrated in the following variations:

A) 31 . . . Kc7 32. Qa5 + .
B) 31 . . . Qc7 32. Rc1.
C) 31 . . . Qe7 32. Bb6!.
D) 31 . . . Qe6 32. Qd2.

White closes in to kill with **31. Qa5.**

Q: What's the threat?

For starters, 32. Rc3 + (or Rc1 +). If Black answers 32 . . . Kd7, the 33. Rc7 + would rapier the Queen. Note how White waited until just the right moment before bringing his Queen into the fray. When a game moves out of the realm of strategy into the arena of tactics, it's time to commit heavy artillery.

Black gambles with **31 . . . Nc4 + .**

Q: Does Black really expect to win White's Queen?

Hardly. He knows White will play the forced move 32. bxc4. Black abandons his obstreperous Knight to seal the c-file.

White plays the forced **32. bxc4.**

Q: How does this capture change the category of White's d-pawn?

Before 32. bxc4, White's d-pawn would be termed a *passed pawn,* as no enemy pawns could stop its march to the promised land. It was an *isolated* passed pawn, however, for there were no friendly pawns on adjacent files to support its advance. After 32. bxc4, the new c-pawn protects the d-pawn, which is now called a *supported* passed pawn.

Black banks on **32 . . . e4.**

Q: *Does this regain the piece?*

This pawn fork wins either the Knight or Rook, but it can't equalize or save the game, as will soon become evident.

White transfers the rook **33. Rb3.**

Q: *Is this the best spot for the Rook?*

Absolutely. The b-file is now the only open passage into Black's position, and White's Rook must occupy it to penetrate to the other side.

Black evens the score materially with **33 . . . exf3.**

Q: *Did Black have a choice?*

None whatever. Having sacrificed his Knight on c4 two moves earlier, this is the only way to regain the material. If he doesn't even up the material, he will eventually lose anyway.

White destroys with **34. Qc5 + .**

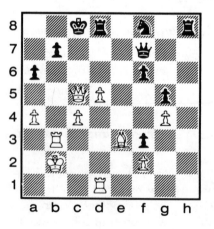

Q: *Is there any reasonable answer to this check?*

No. Whatever Black does he must lose material. Here are some variations:

A) 34 . . . Kd7 35. Rxb7+ wins the Queen.

B) 34 . . . Kb8 35. Qa7+ Kc8 36. Qa8+ Kd7 37. Rxb7+ Ke8 38. Qxd8+ Kxd8 39. Rxf7 wins a Rook.

C) 34 . . . Qc7 35. Qxc7+ Kxc7 36. Bb6+ Kc8 37. Bxd8 Kxd8 38. Rxb7, and White has won a Rook and pawn for a Bishop.

BLACK RESIGNS

POSTSCRIPT

Why does Rogers give up? Can't he grit his teeth for a little while just to see if his Russian opponent plays the correct moves? In such forced situations, where every move is direct and plain—either a check or capture—there's no doubt that White will see what to do. For a Soviet grandmaster, or any master for that matter, the winning moves would be child's play to find.

The only justification for playing on in hopeless positions at the grandmaster level is time trouble—if the superior side is extremely short of time. This game, for example, was played at the rate of 40 moves in two-and-a-half hours for each player. If Dolmatov had but seconds on his clock to reach the 40th move, then of course Rogers might have played on. He could still have won on time forfeit, regardless of how bad his position was. That Rogers did resign here is the best indication that Dolmatov was not in time trouble.

ALEKHINE: The inability of an experienced player to deal with the clock should be considered as grave a fault as miscalculation.

As for the game, it was a positional blowout. Black was in a pressure cooker throughout, thanks to his time-wasting Queen move in the opening. White increased his spatial advantage gradually, found just the right placements for his pieces, and waited until everything was ready before the final invasion. He made sure, for example, not to utilize the Queen until its use was timely. Depleted of space, counterplay, and thus hope, Black's continued resistance would have almost convinced us that . . .

> **DOSTOYEVSKY:** Man is a frivolous, specious creature, and like a chessplayer cares more for the process of attaining his goal than for the goal itself.

GRANDMASTER GLOSSARY

Alekhine, Alexander (1892–1946)—World Champion from 1927–35 and from 1937 to his death. Dethroned the "invincible" Jose Raoul Capablanca in their 1927 thirty-four game match in Buenos Aires to become history's fourth title-holder. A controversial figure because of his supposed Nazi leanings, perhaps the most gifted attacking player of all time.

Belyavsky, Alexander (born 1953)—World Junior Champion in 1973. Leading grandmaster who was defeated by Kasparov in the quarter-finals of the 1983 Candidates cycle.

Botvinnik, Mikhail (born 1911)—Three times world champion: 1948–57, 1958–60, and 1961–63. The "father" of the Soviet school and the most respected living chess authority, he is in the forefront of the development of computer chess and was the teacher of Gary Kasparov.

Bronstein, David (born 1924)—Vanguard innovator and top player who drew the 1951 world championship match with Botvinnik (Botvinnik kept the title). His book on the 1953 Zurich interzonal is considered the best of the genre.

Cebalo, Miso (born 1945)—Grandmaster who tied for first in the 1985 Yugoslavian Championship.

Cernin, Alexander (born 1960)—Grandmaster and co-champion of the Soviet Union in 1985. He won the right to enter the Candidates tournament by defeating Gavrikov in a match.

Chigorin, Mikhail (1850–1908)—One of the four or five best players in the world in the latter part of the nineteenth century. A founder of the Russian School, Chigorin lost two world championship matches to Wilhelm Steinitz, the first World Champion.

Dolmatov, Sergei (born 1959)—World Junior Champion in 1978. A grandmaster and student of Mark Dvoretsky, Russia's foremost chess trainer.

Estrin, Yakov (born 1923)—Preeminent openings theoretician and teacher, he has authored numerous textbooks and treatises on the opening phase.

Gavrikov, Victor (born 1957)—Soviet grandmaster and former co-champion of Russia in 1985.

Grekov, Nikolai—Russian master who finished second to Alekhine in Moscow tournaments in 1919 and 1920. An author best known for his work on Mikhail Chigorin, he was Russia's greatest player before the Revolution. Founded Shakhmaty Bulletin in 1922.

Karpov, Anatoly (1951–)—Controversial twelfth champion of the world (1975–85), who captured the crown by default when America's Bobby Fischer failed to defend his title in 1975. A highly successful competitor, he's won numerous international tournaments and two championship match defenses against Viktor Korchnoi. In 1985 his match with Gary Kasparov was halted by the president of the world chess federation when Karpov seemed on the verge of defeat. The second meeting of the two was held later that year and resulted in Karpov's dethronement. Still up there with the best.

Kasparov, Gary (1963–)—The youngest world champion in history, he assumed that role when at age twenty-two he toppled Anatoly Karpov in their second match in 1985, winning five to three. His dynamic attacking style and innovative approach to the game have flowered a chess renaissance around the world. The most spectacular player to emerge since the U.S.'s Bobby Fischer.

Keres, Paul (1916–75)—Brilliant attacker and commentator, he finished second in the world championship cycle four times. Along with Victor Korchnoi, he is one of the strongest players never to become world champion. Cowinner, along with America's Reuben Fine, of the 1938 AVRO tournament, perhaps the greatest tournament of all time.

Koblentz, Alexander—Noted trainer and teacher who was a second for World Champion Mikhail Tal in two world championship matches.

Korchnoi, Victor (1931–)—Russia's most famous chess defector (1977), for ten years he was the second highest rated player in the world behind Anatoly Karpov until the rise of Gary Kasparov. He's won many premier events, lost three matches to Karpov (two for the title and two by only one point), and remains a feared world class fighter.

Kotov, Alexander (1913–81)—Grandmaster who trumpeted the merits of the Soviet school, best known for his books and writings, many of which are vitiated by their inclusion of crude propaganda. In 1952 he won the interzonal tournament, starting a Soviet victory record that lasted for eighteen years until it was broken by Bobby Fischer.

Lisitzin, Georgi (1909–72)—A fierce competitor and international master, he won the championship of Leningrad three times and the Soviet Trade Union Championship of 1936. He is best remembered for his textbooks on strategy and tactics, which are standards throughout Russia.

Makogonov, Vladimir (1904–)—A reasonably strong international master, he is best known as an analyst, having functioned as Vassily Smyslov's second in the 1957 world championship match with Botvinnik.

Miles, Anthony (1955–   )—In 1976 he became the first British international grandmaster and has maintained his position as one of the world's ten best players since then. In 1986 he was overwhelmed in his match with champion Kasparov, losing five of six games and drawing one.

Nogueiras, Jesus (born 1959)—Cuban grandmaster and recent candidate for the world championship.

Panczyk, K.—A Polish international master who earned his title in 1984.

Petrosian, Tigran (1929–84)—World champion from 1963 to 1969. He won the title by topping Botvinnik in

1963. He defended it successfully against Boris Spassky in 1966, but lost it to Spassky in 1969. One of his most memorable achievements was beating Bobby Fischer in the second game of their 1971 Candidates Match, halting Fischer's record-breaking streak of twenty consecutive international victories. Though Fischer won the match by four points, Petrosian put up heroic resistance.

Petrov, Alexander (1794–1867)—Russia's first great player, he has been immortalized in the opening that bear's his name, the Petrov Defense (1. e4 e5 2. Nf3 Nf6).

Polugaevsky, Lev (1934–)—A prominent grandmaster and theoretician, he has achieved innumerable international successes. In the Candidates cycle, he lost to Karpov in 1974, but defeated Brazil's Henrique Mecking in 1977. He has contributed significantly to the development of the Najdorf Sicilian (1. e4 c5 2. Nf3 d6 3. d4 cxd4 4. Nxd4 Nf6 5. Nc3 a6).

Rogers, Ian (born 1960)—Australia's leading grandmaster and a noted authority on opening theory.

Shereshevsky, M.I.—Famed trainer who has modelled his teaching on the program of Mark Dvoretsky.

Smyslov, Vassily (1921–)—Defeated Botvinnik in 1958 to become the seventh world champion. In three title matches with Botvinnik, after sixty-nine games, he was ahead by one point against his renowned countryman. Only Gary Kasparov could prevent him, at the age of sixty-two, from earning a championship match with Karpov, thus stopping Smyslov from becoming the oldest world championship competitor in history.

Spassky, Boris (1937–)—The eleventh world champion, he defeated Tigran Petrosian in 1969 to gain the title. But he will be forever known as the man who lost to Bobby Fischer in Reykjavik, Iceland in 1972 in the most publicized chess match ever held. He has since emigrated to the West, where he lives in Paris with his French-born wife. Still an awesome player, capable of beating anyone.

Tal, Mikhail (1936–)—World champion 1960–61. The world's most famous chess journalist, his name recalls brilliant, speculative attacks and unfathomable moves. At his height, a powerful attacking player with a unique style.

Vaganjan, Rafael (born 1951)—An international grandmaster at nineteen, he has been a top competitor since the early 1970s and a candidate for the world championship.

Vainstein,—A noted critic and commentator from the Russian town of Tashkent.

Yusupov, Artur (born 1960)—World Junior Champion in 1977. A student of Mark Dvoretsky, a candidate for the world championship, and one of the three or four best players in the world.

INDEX

215

About the Author

Bruce Pandolfini, a U.S. National Chess Master, gained prominence as an analyst on PBS's live telecast of the Fischer-Spassky championship match in 1972. In due course, he lectured widely on chess and in 1978 was chosen to deliver the Bobby Fischer Chess Lectures at the University of Alabama in Birmingham. His first book, *Let's Play Chess,* appeared in 1980. The author is a *Chess Life* magazine consulting editor, for which he writes the monthly "ABCs of Chess." He is the author of *Bobby Fischer's Outrageous Chess Moves, One-Move Chess by the Champions, Principles of the New Chess, The ABCs of Chess,* and *Kasparov's Winning Chess Tactics.* He has also written columns for *Time-Video,* the *Litchfield County Times,* and *Physician's Travel and Meeting Guide.*

As a chess teacher, he's been on the faculty of the New School for Social Research since 1973, and currently conducts chess classes at Browning, Trinity, and the Little Red School House in New York City. With U.S. Champion Lev Alburt, he has developed special children's programs sponsored by the American Chess Foundation. The director of the world famous Manhattan Chess Club at Carnegie Hall, Pandolfini visited the USSR in the fall of 1984 to study Soviet teaching methods and observe the controversial championship match between Anatoly Karpov and Gary Kasparov.

FIRESIDE **C**HESS **L**IBRARY

**Just a reminder about the treasure of chess books from Fireside,
for all players from beginners to advanced chess masters!**

NEW TITLES:

RUSSIAN CHESS
Bruce Pandolfini
144 pgs, 61984-5, $6.95

**KASPAROV'S WINNING CHESS
TACTICS**
Bruce Pandolfini
208 pgs, 61985-3, $6.95

ABC'S OF CHESS
Bruce Pandolfini
128 pgs, 61982-9, $6.95

LET'S PLAY CHESS
Bruce Pandolfini
192 pgs, 61983-7, $6.95

CHESS BACKLIST:

CHESS FOR BEGINNERS
I.A. Horowitz
134 pgs, 21184-6, $5.95

CHESS OPENINGS
I.A. Horowitz
792 pgs, 20553-6, $16.95

CHESS TRAPS
I.A. Horowitz & Fred Reinfeld
250 pgs, 21041-6, $6.95

HOW TO THINK AHEAD IN CHESS
I.A. Horowitz & Fred Reinfeld
274 pgs, 21138-2, $6.95

THE CHESS COMPANION
Irving Chernev
288 pgs, 21651-1, $9.95

CHESS THE EASY WAY
Reuben Fine
186 pgs, 0-346-12323-2, $5.95

**THE MOST INSTRUCTIVE GAMES
OF CHESS EVER PLAYED**
Irving Chernev
286 pgs, 21536-1, $8.95

PRINCIPLES OF THE NEW CHESS
Bruce Pandolfini
144 pgs, 60719-7, $6.95 (Available
March '86)

AN INVITATION TO CHESS
Irving Chernev & Kenneth Harkness
224 pgs, 21270-2, $5.95

LOGICAL CHESS, MOVE BY MOVE
Irving Chernev
250 pgs, 21135-8, $7.95

WINNING CHESS
Irving Chernev & Fred Reinfeld
236 pgs, 21114-5, $7.95

**HOW TO WIN IN THE CHESS
OPENINGS**
I.A. Horowitz
192 pgs, 0-346-12445-X, $5.95

**BOBBY FISCHER'S OUTRAGEOUS
CHESS MOVES**
Bruce Pandolfini
128 pgs, 60609-3, $6.95

**THE 1,000 BEST SHORT GAMES
OF CHESS**
Irving Chernev
562 pgs, 53801-2, $7.95

THE FIRESIDE BOOK OF CHESS
Irving Chernev & Fred Reinfeld
406 pgs, 21221-4, $8.95

**ONE MOVE CHESS BY THE
CHAMPIONS**
Bruce Pandolfini
128 pgs, 60608-5, $6.95

Send order to:
Simon & Schuster Mail Order Dept. CB
200 Old Tappan Road
Old Tappan, NJ 07675

Total costs all books ordered _____
Postage and handling __$1.50__
New York residents add applicable sales tax _____
Enclosed is my payment for books ordered _____
(check or money order ONLY)

Ship to:
Name _____

Address _____

City _____ State _____ Zip code _____